THE GLASGOW PENGUINS

A YEAR IN OUR LIVES

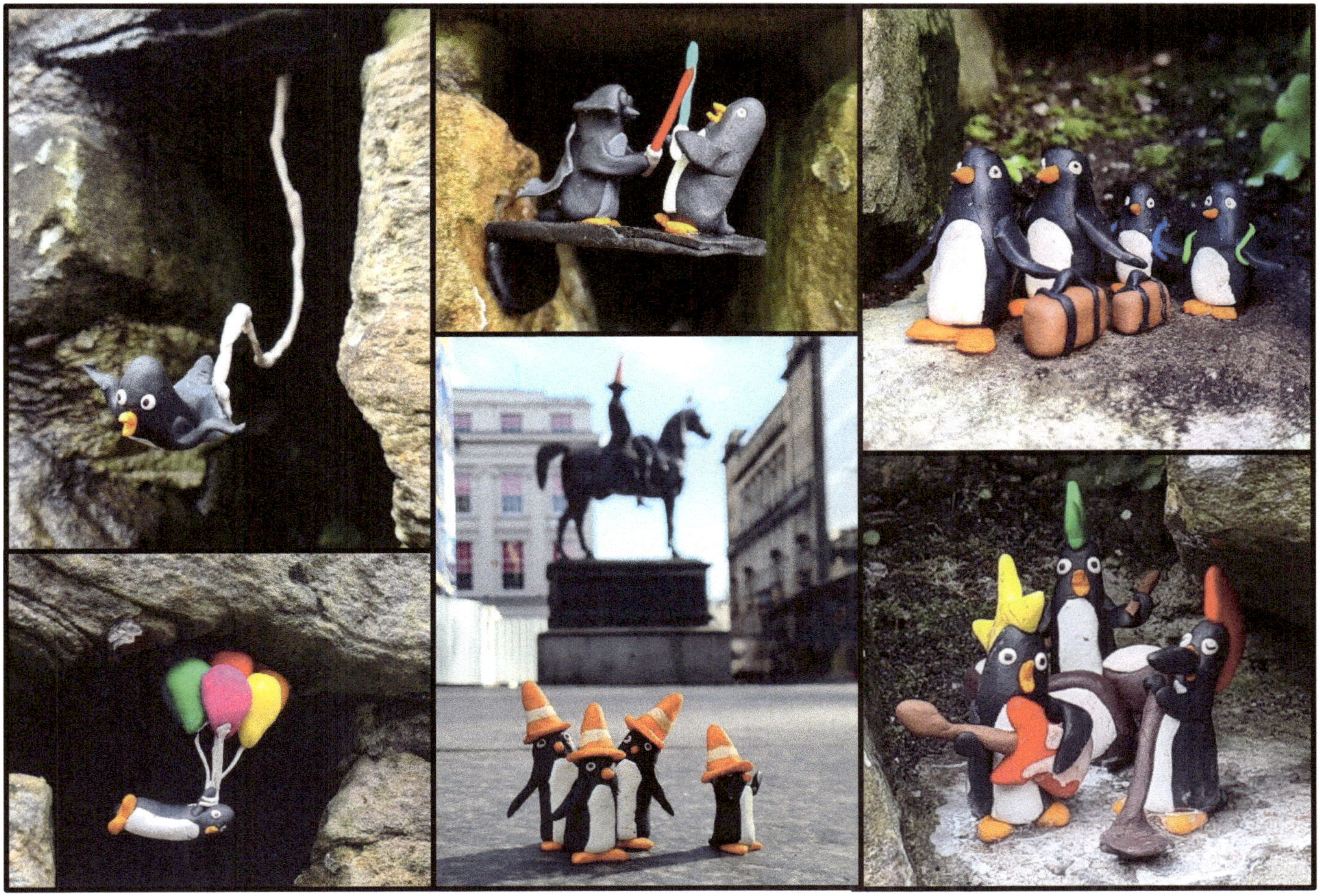

The Glasgow Penguins

Pictish Beast Publications

ISBN - 978-1-909832-87-9
Published by Pictish Beast Publications, Glasgow, UK.
Published in the United Kingdom
First Printing: 2024. First Edition, Hardback.

www.PictishBeastPublications.com

In February 2023, a small group of penguins, forced to leave Antarctica due to the changing climate, found themselves a new home in the nooks and crannies of an old stone wall on the banks of the River Kelvin in the West End of Scotland's largest, and coolest, city.

Written by one young penguin, this book documents their first year in a city they have come to know and love, and which, in turn, has come to know and love them.

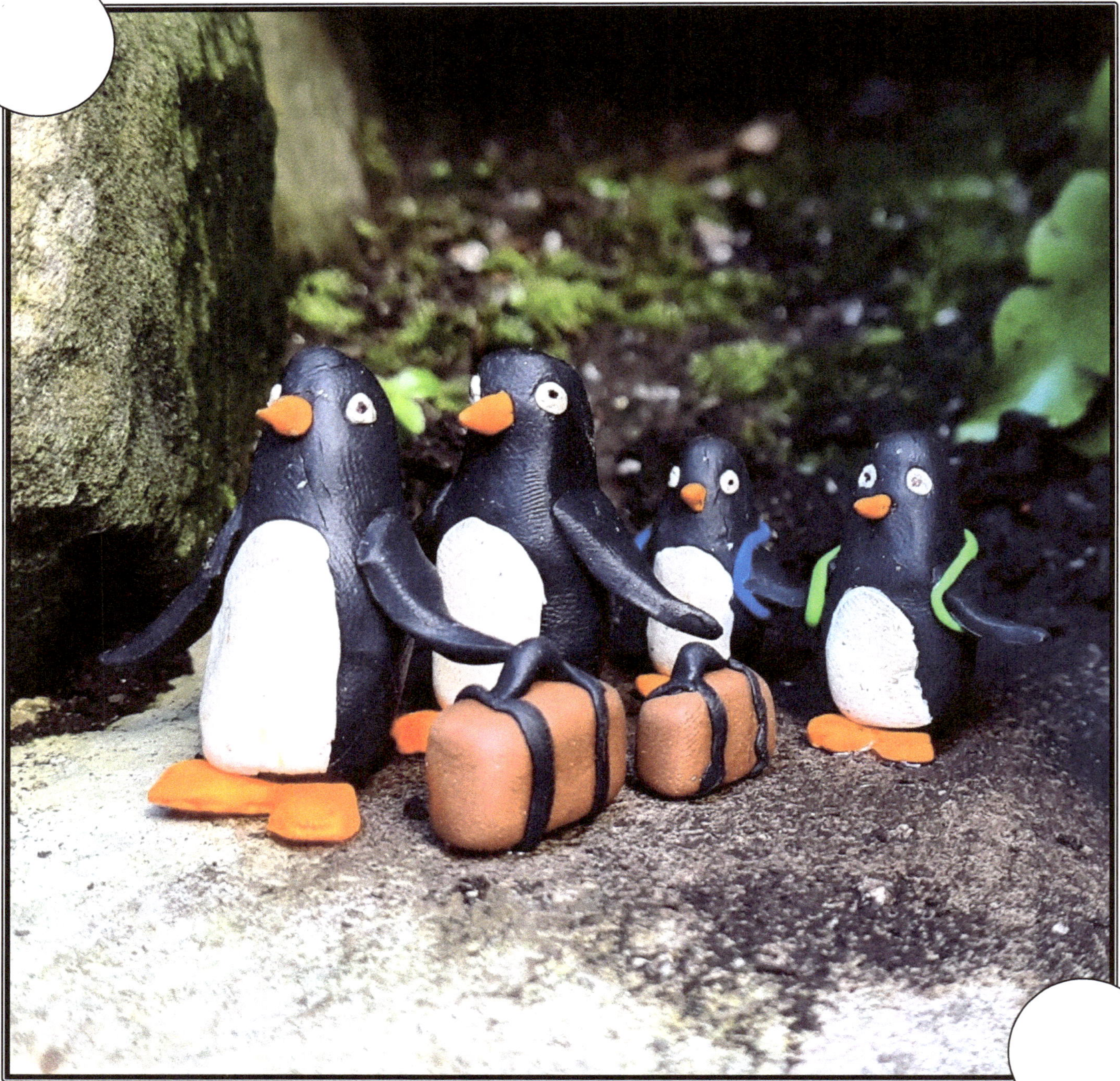

25th February 2023

When we had to leave our home in Antarctica because it was getting too warm and the ice was melting, we didn't know where we would end up. Then Mum heard about a place called Glasgow, and it sounded so cool, so we decided we'd move there.

This is how my family and me looked on the day we arrived in Glasgow - I'm the one with the green backpack. We found a nice old wall with lots of nooks and crannies where we could live along with the other members of our colony.

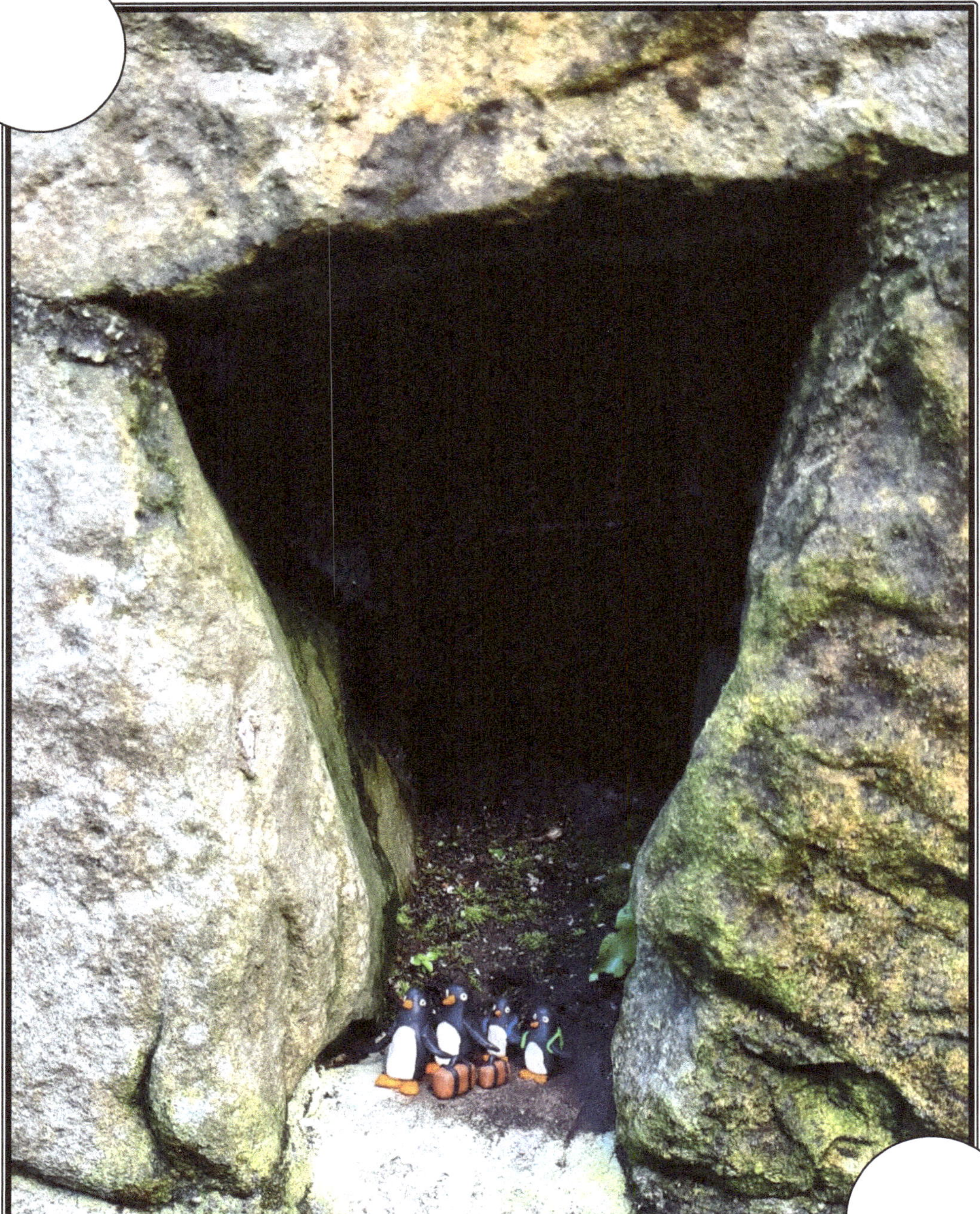

28th February 2023

The wall we moved into is
beside a very nice river called the
Kelvin which runs through the West End
of Glasgow. It's surrounded by trees,
and there's the ruins of an old
mill just in front of it.

This is the hole in the wall where we
set up our new home. We call ourselves
the Penguins in the Wall, but everyone
just calls us ...

...The Glasgow Penguins!

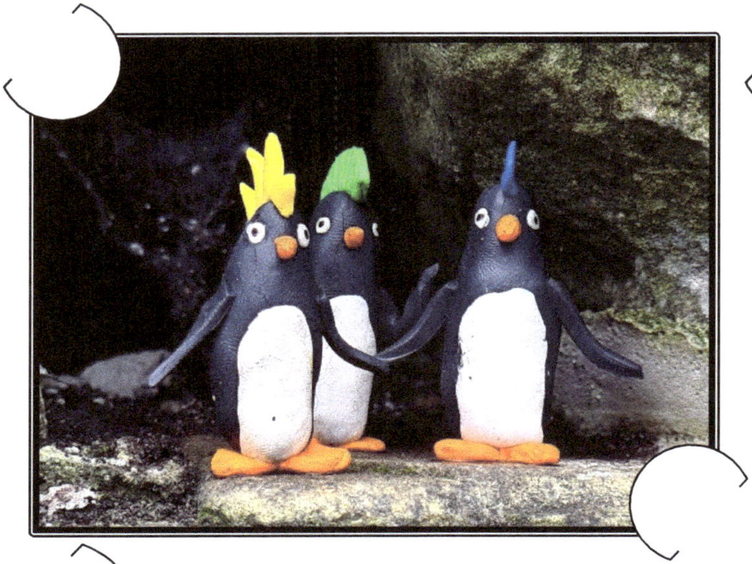

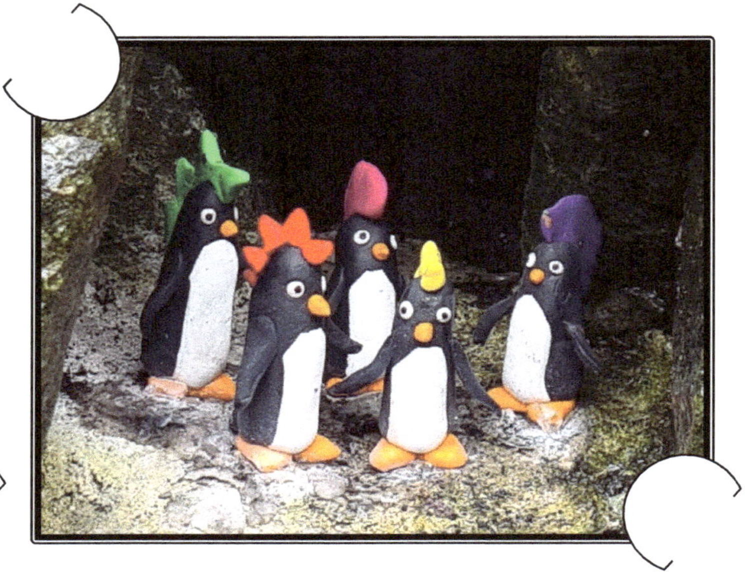

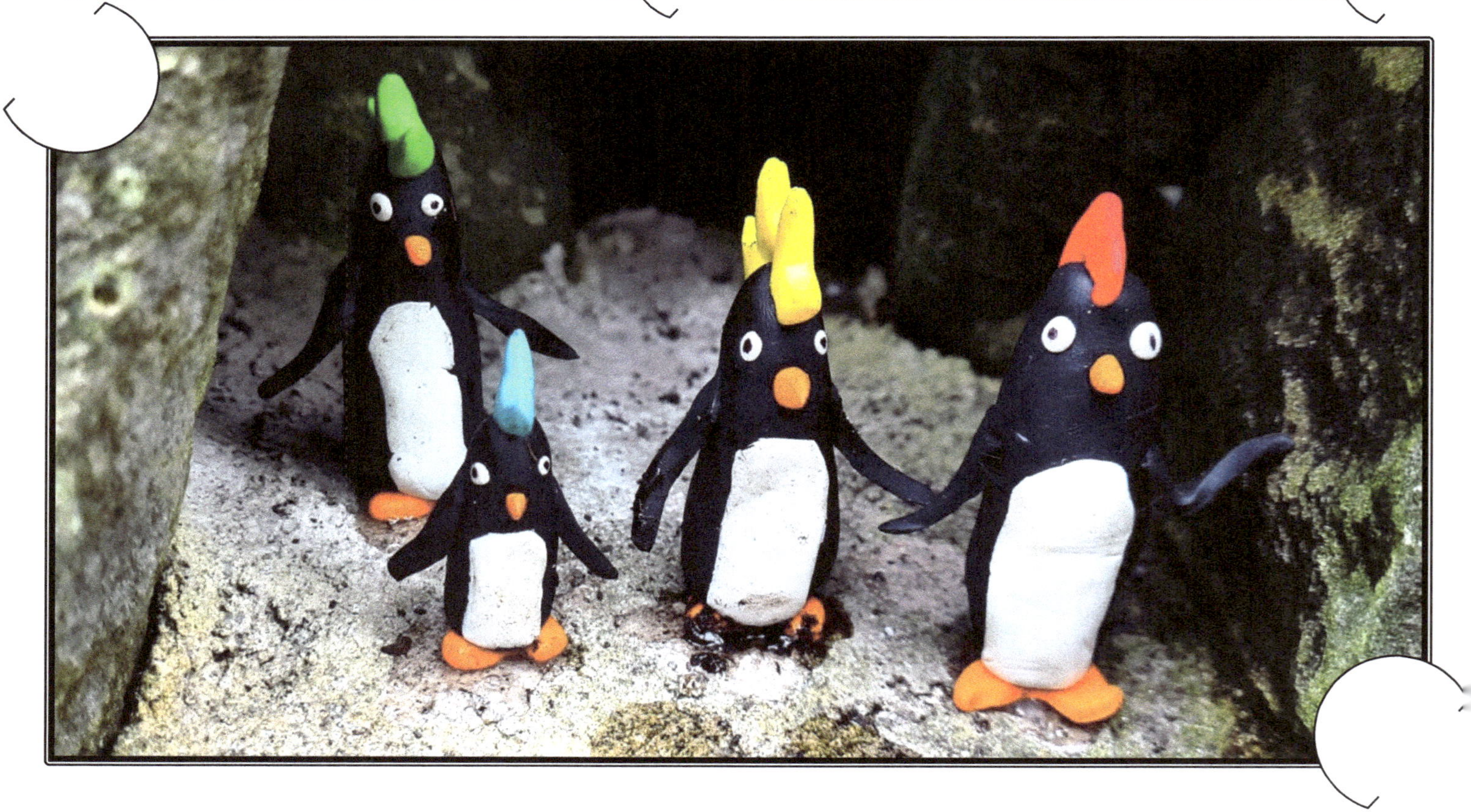

3rd March 2023

Our family are not the only penguins in the wall. Next door to us are some punks. Sometimes there's only a few of them and sometimes there's quite a lot. They might look a bit different, but they're really very nice. They even help look after my Little Brother from time to time.

He's the one with the blue hair in the bottom photograph. Don't worry, that's not his real hair, it's just a wig Mum made for him because he wanted to look like the rest of them.

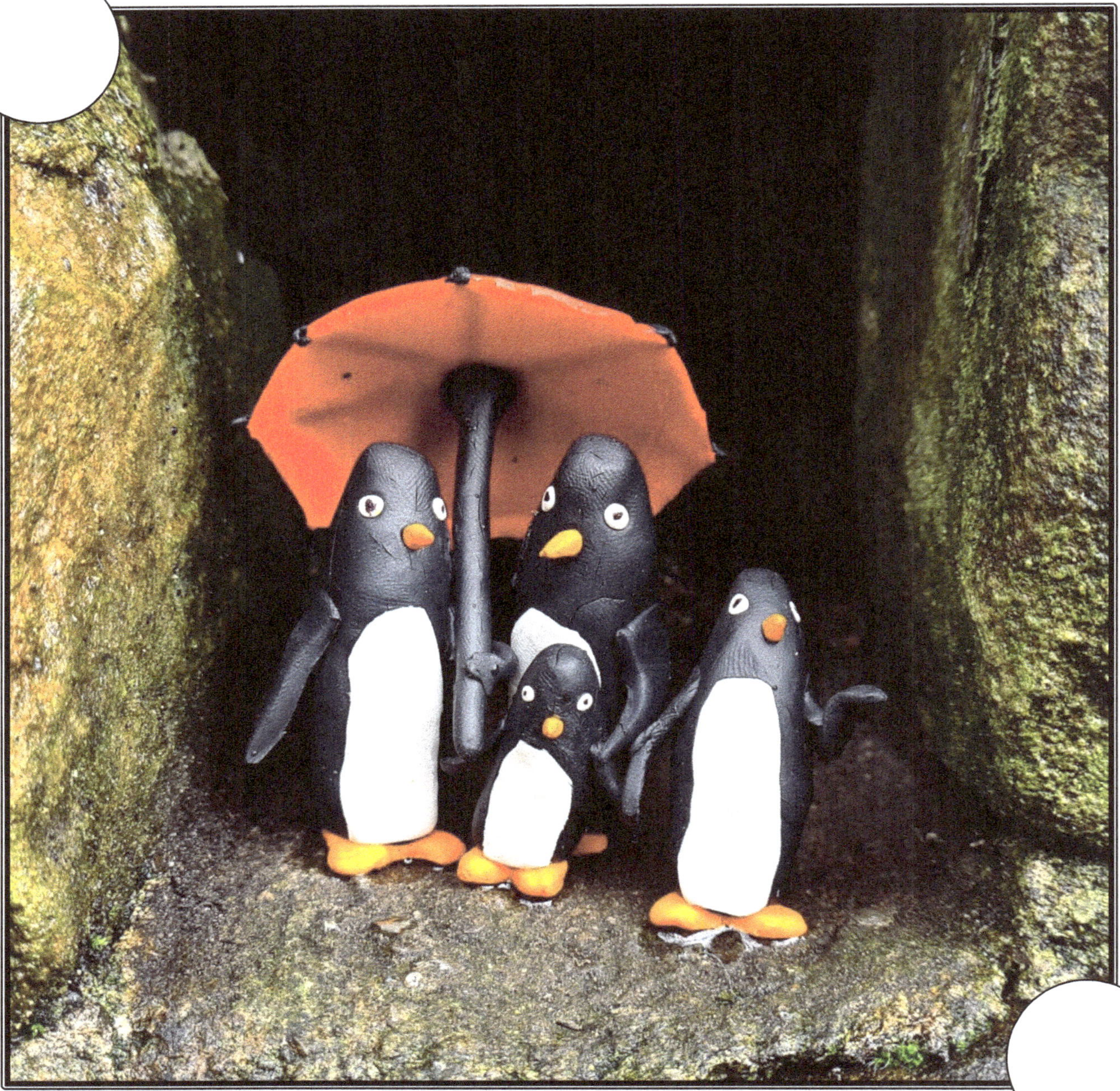

8th March 2023

Glasgow is great,
but sometimes it rains
rather a lot!

My teacher
calls it Tinseltown
in the Rain.

I get the rain bit,
but I don't know why she
calls it Tinseltown!

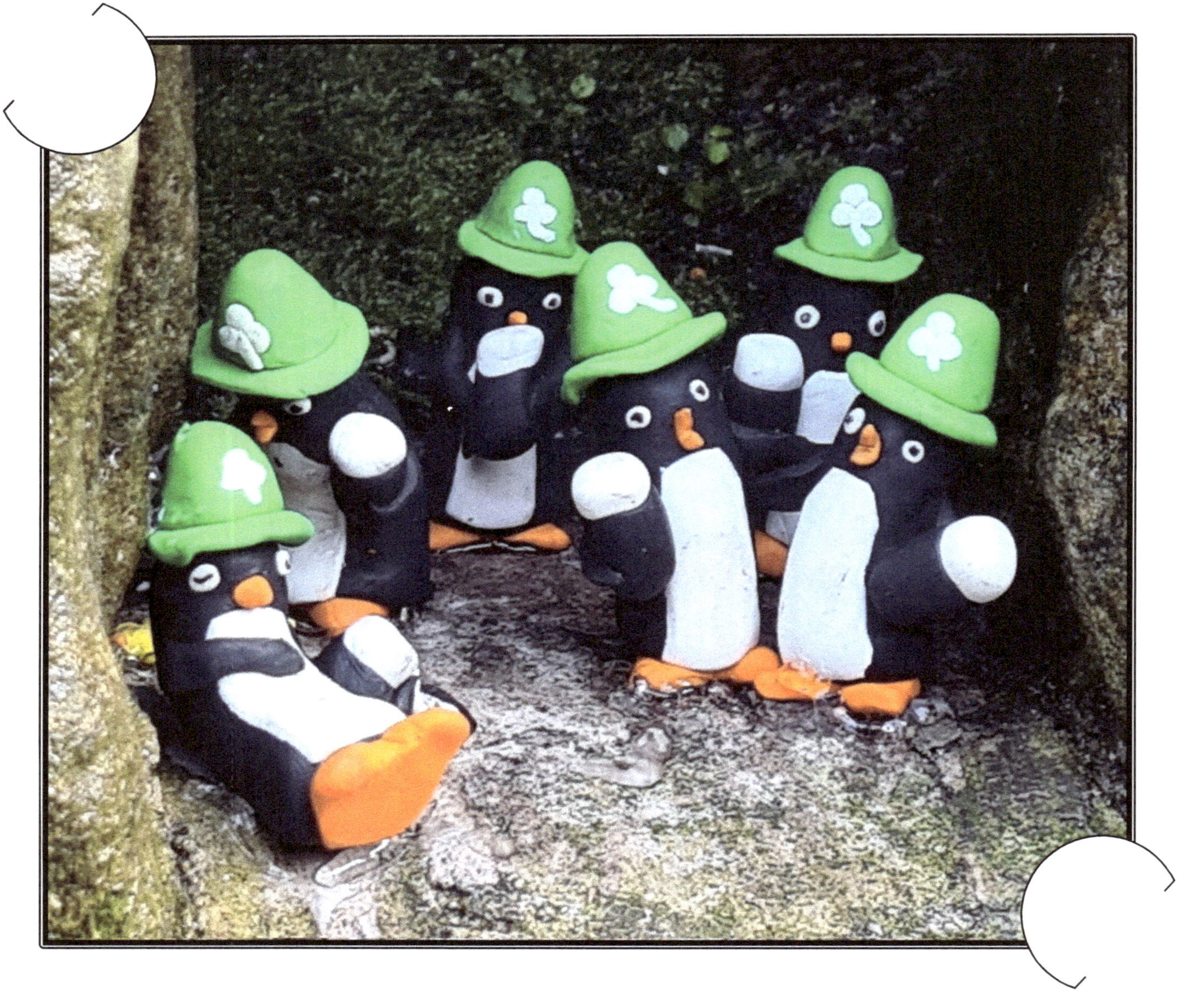

17th March 2023

Today is Saint Patrick's Day,
and a lot of people seem to celebrate it in Glasgow. Dad went out with some of his friends. He's the one on the right drinking Guinness and singing very loudly out of tune. He was very hungover the next day!

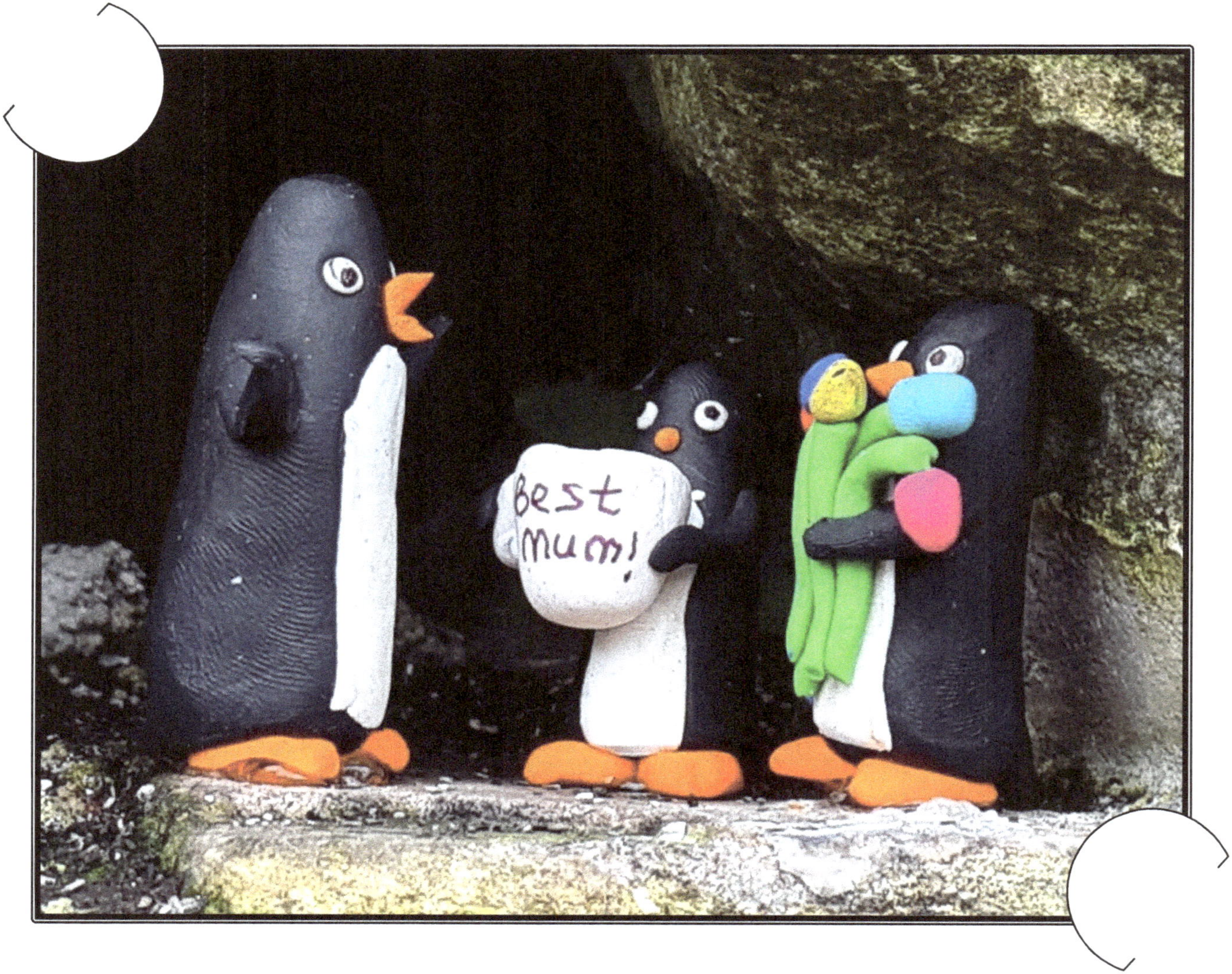
Best
mum!

19th March 2023

As it's Mother's Day here in our new home, me and my Little Brother decided to surprise our Mum with some presents. I picked her some flowers and my brother got her a mug. We didn't wrap them because wrapping presents with flippers is much more difficult than you might think!

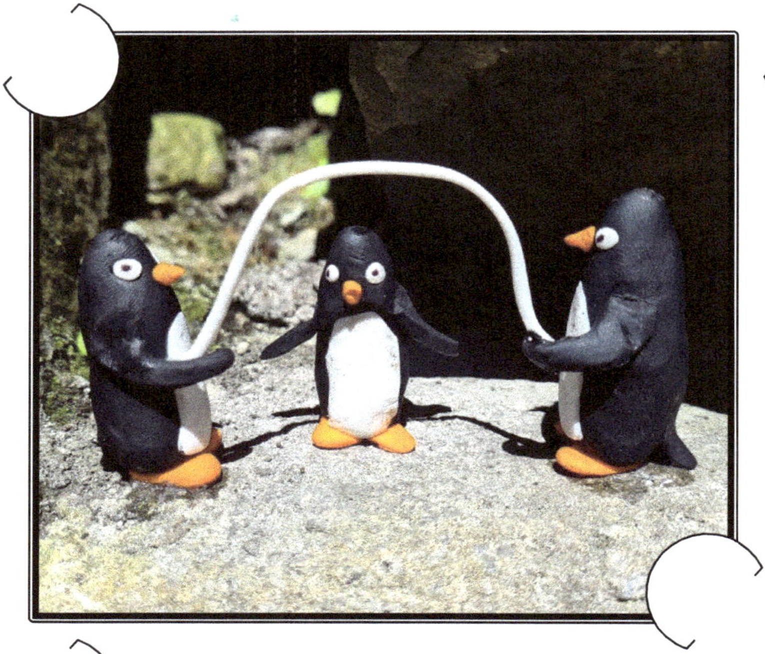

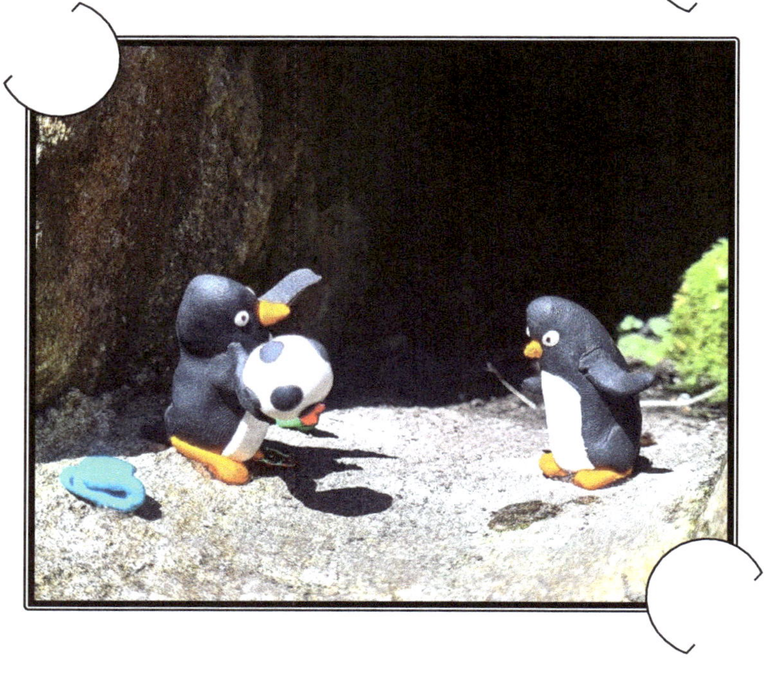

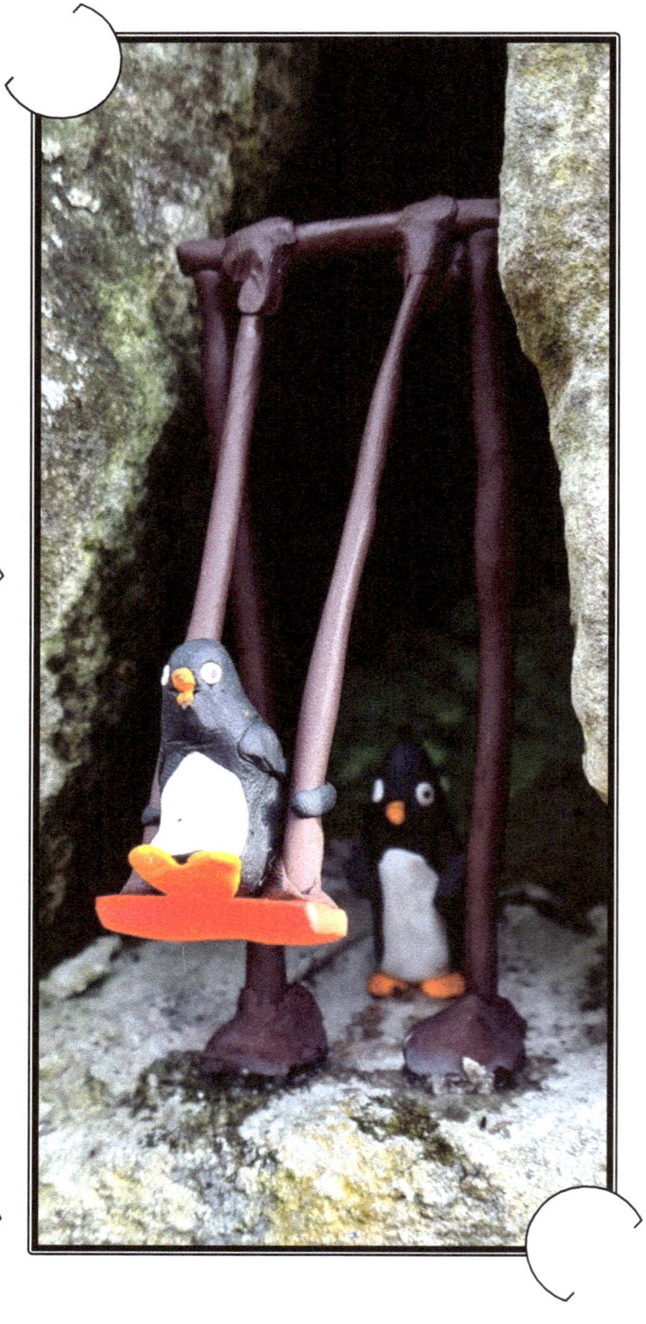

25th March 2023

Me and my brother like to go out and play when I get home from school. My Little Brother likes to skip, while I like playing football with my friends. We both like playing on the swing which Mum built for us.

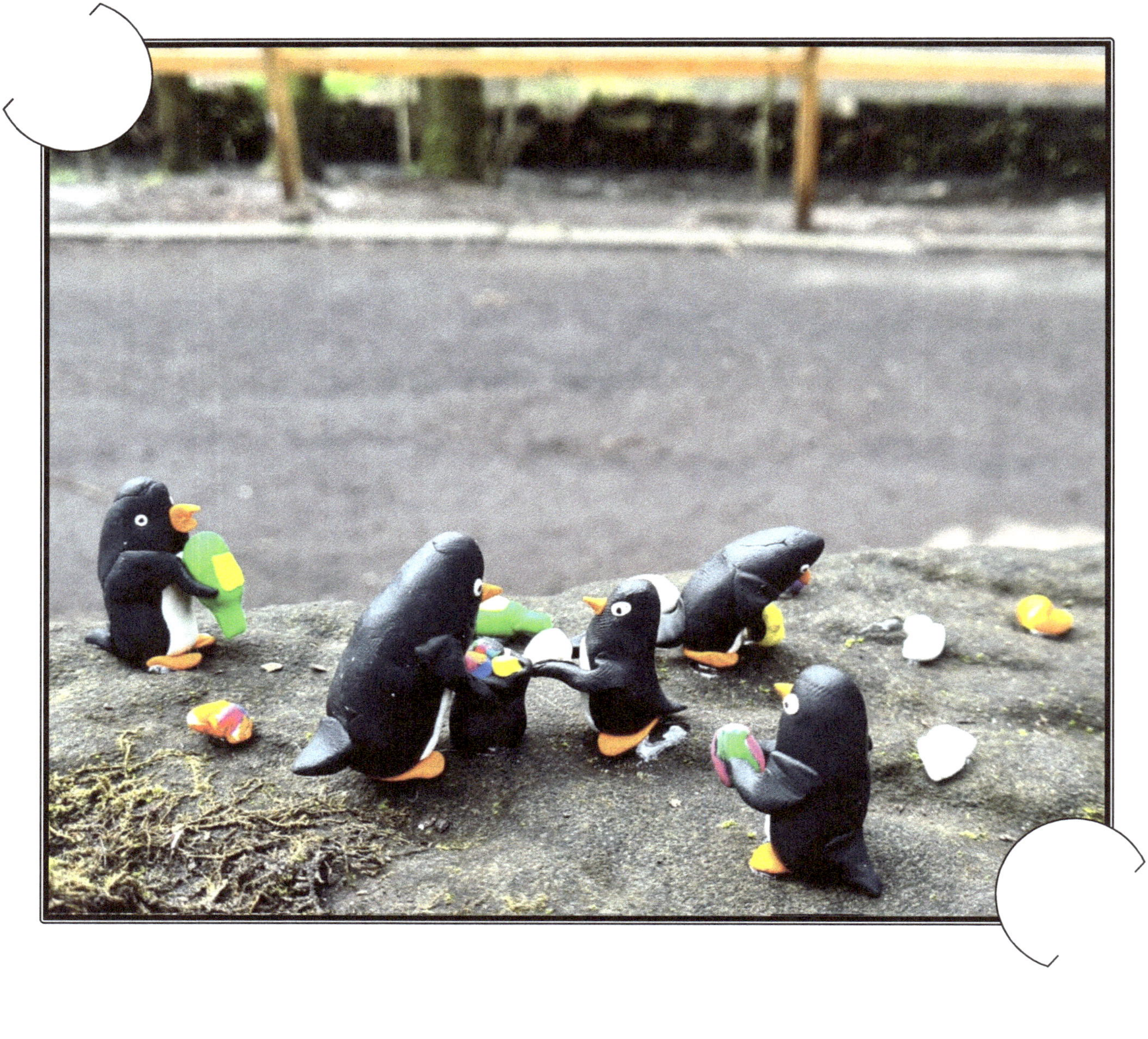

2nd April 2023

We might be penguins rather than wombles, but we still like to help keep Glasgow tidy! It also makes us feel like we're part of the local community.

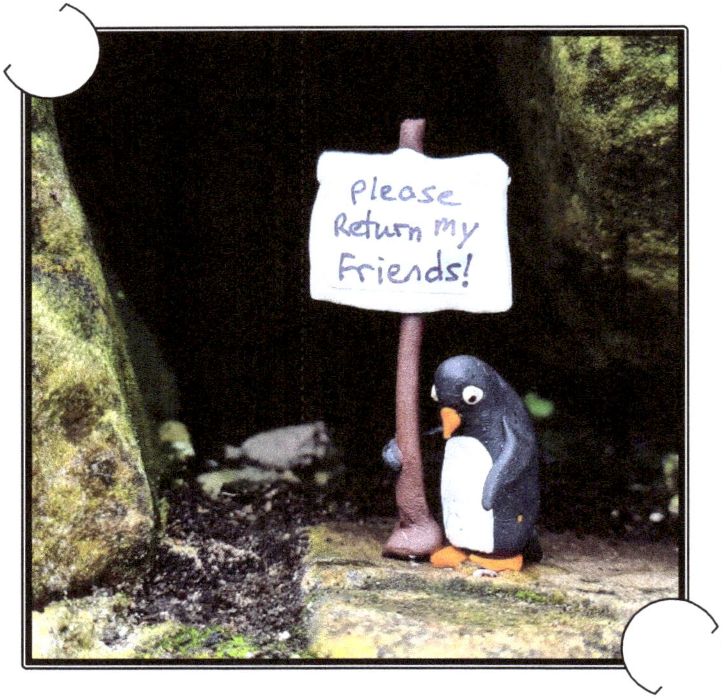
Please Return my Friends!

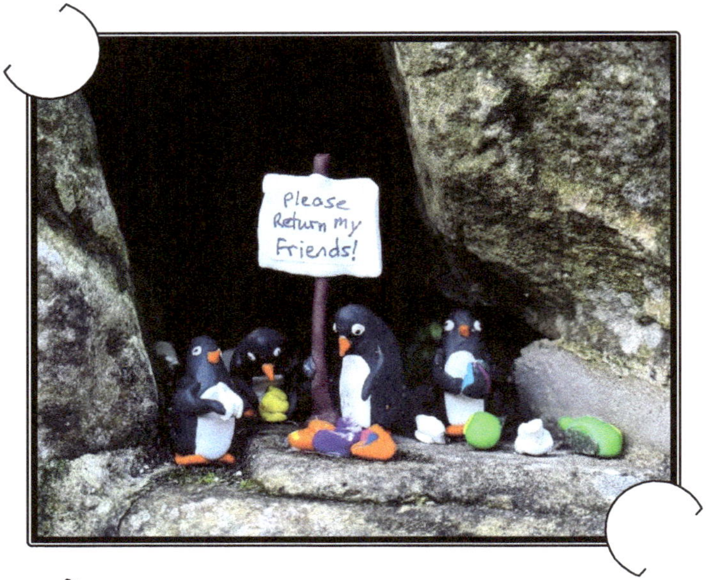
Please Return my Friends!

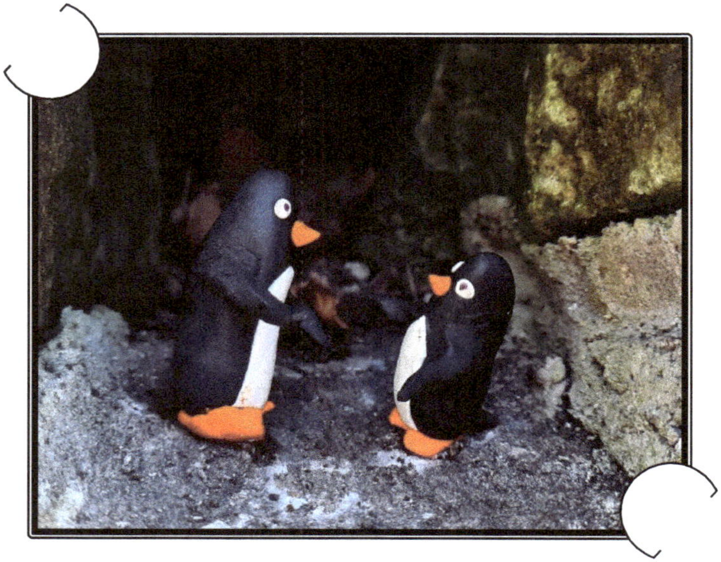

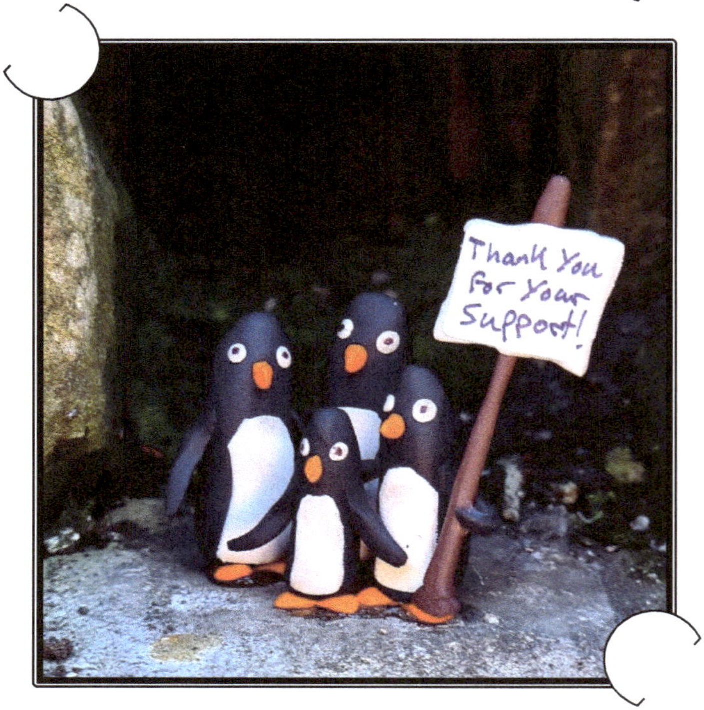
Thank You for Your Support!

5th April 2023

Today was a disaster! Some penguin-nappers targeted our colony and lots of us went missing, including my Mum. I was very upset. I made a sign to help get everyone back. It caused a lot of fuss and even made the papers!

Some made their way home on their own, and some were helped out by local people. It took Mum a bit longer, but finally we were re-united. I was so happy to see her again!

I made another sign to thank everyone for their help.

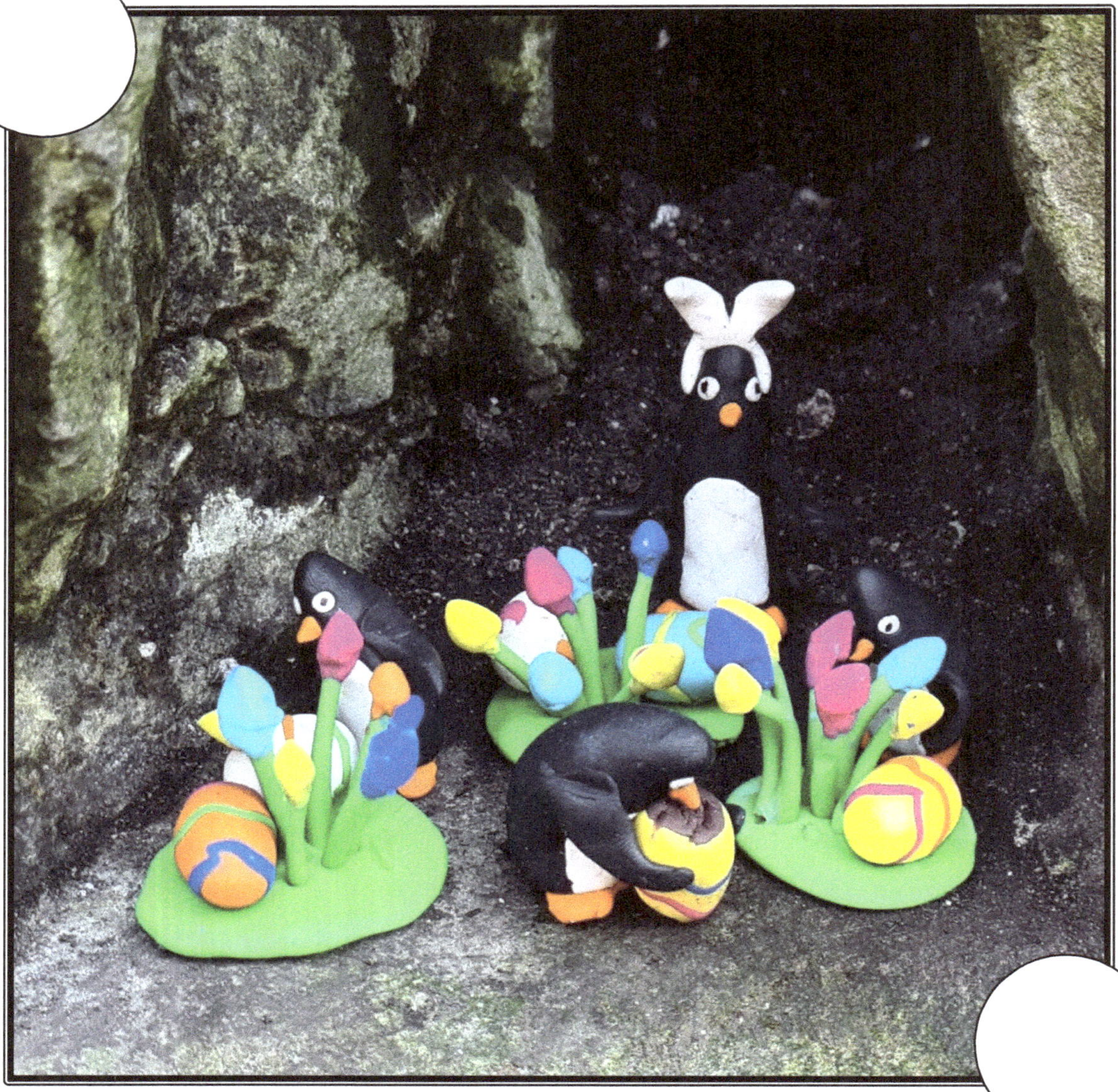

9th April 2023

As today is Easter, Dad dressed up as the Easter Bunny and we had an Easter egg hunt amongst the Spring flowers. I found mine first - I REALLY like chocolate!!!

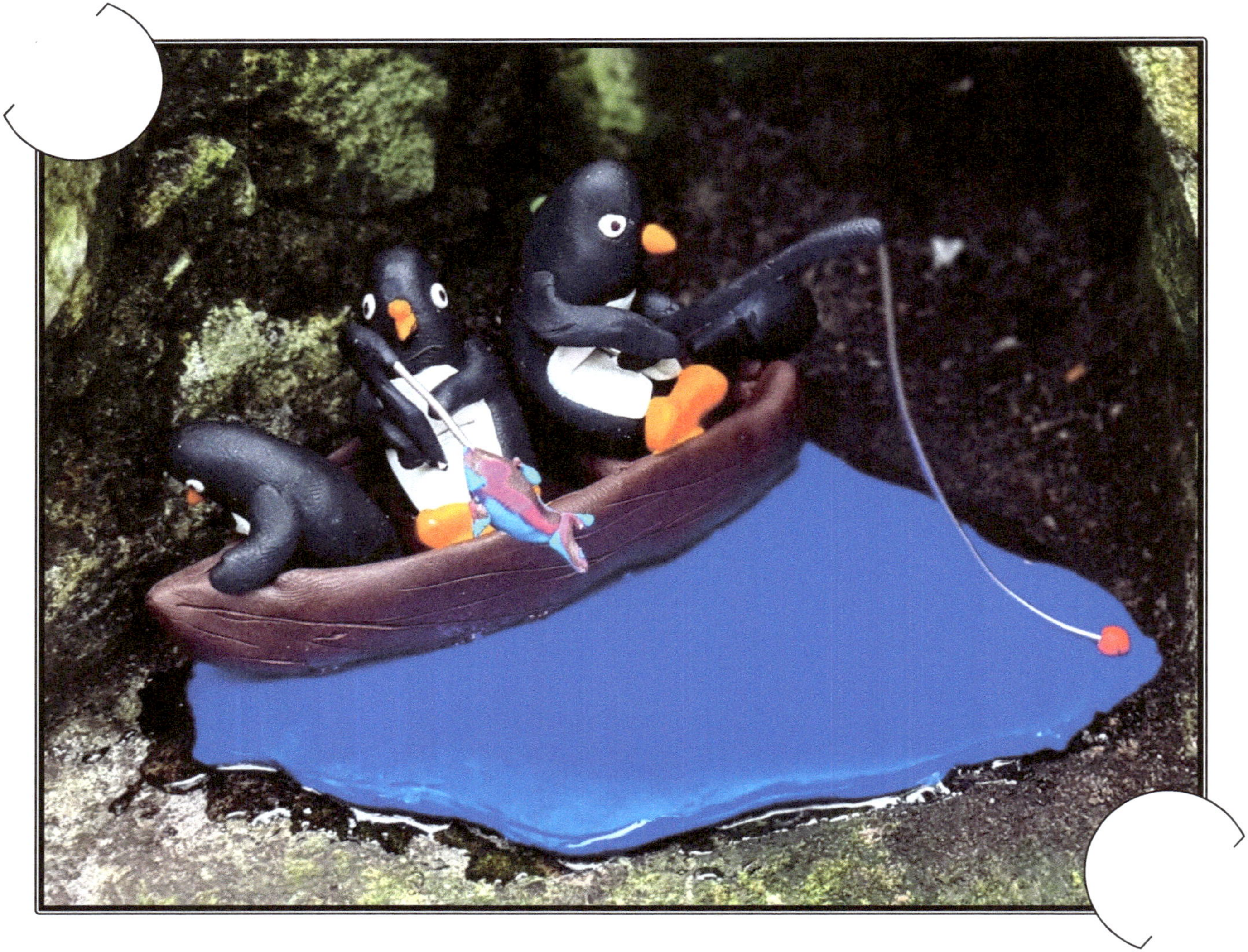

14th April 2023

Whenever we get the time,
me, Dad and my Little Brother like to
go fishing. I always catch more
than anyone else,
even Dad.

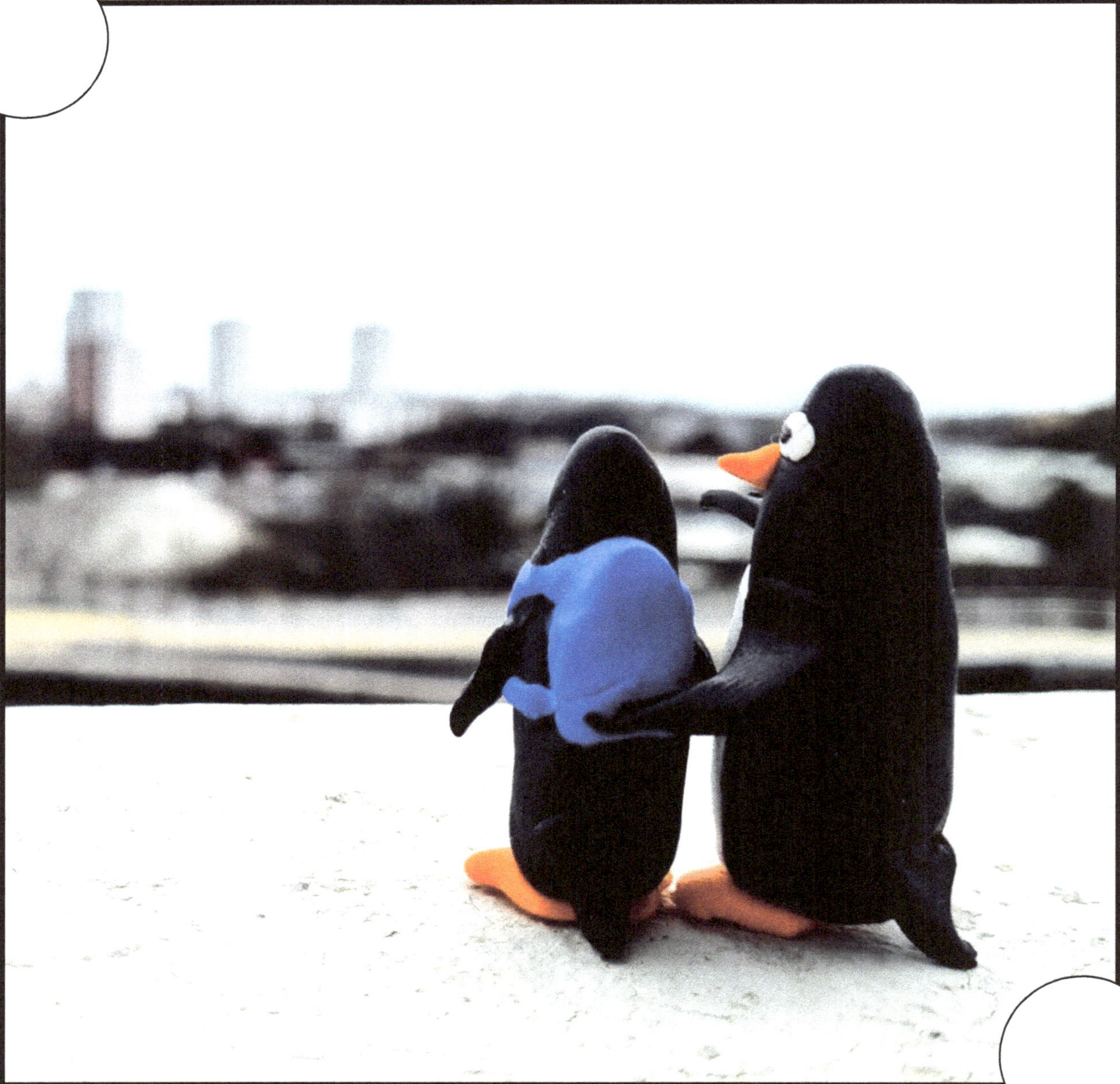

25th April 2023

We've been in Glasgow for
almost two month now, so after school
today me and Dad decided to take a look
around. We waddled up to a place called
Stockingfield Junction where we could look
out across the city. Glasgow's much
bigger than I ever imagined!

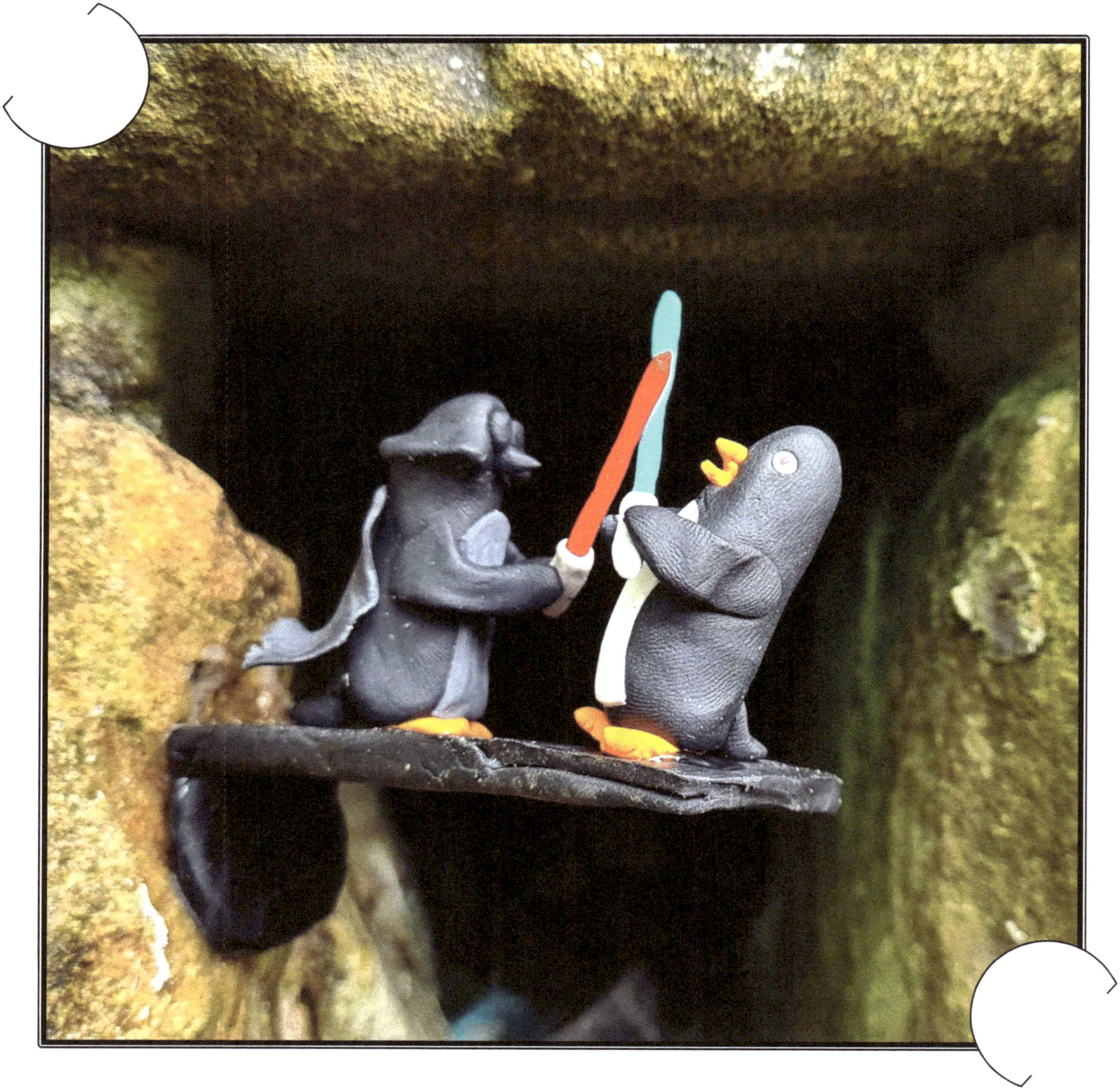

4th May 2023

Look, it is my Father ...
... and me celebrating Star Wars day
- May the 4th be with you!!!!

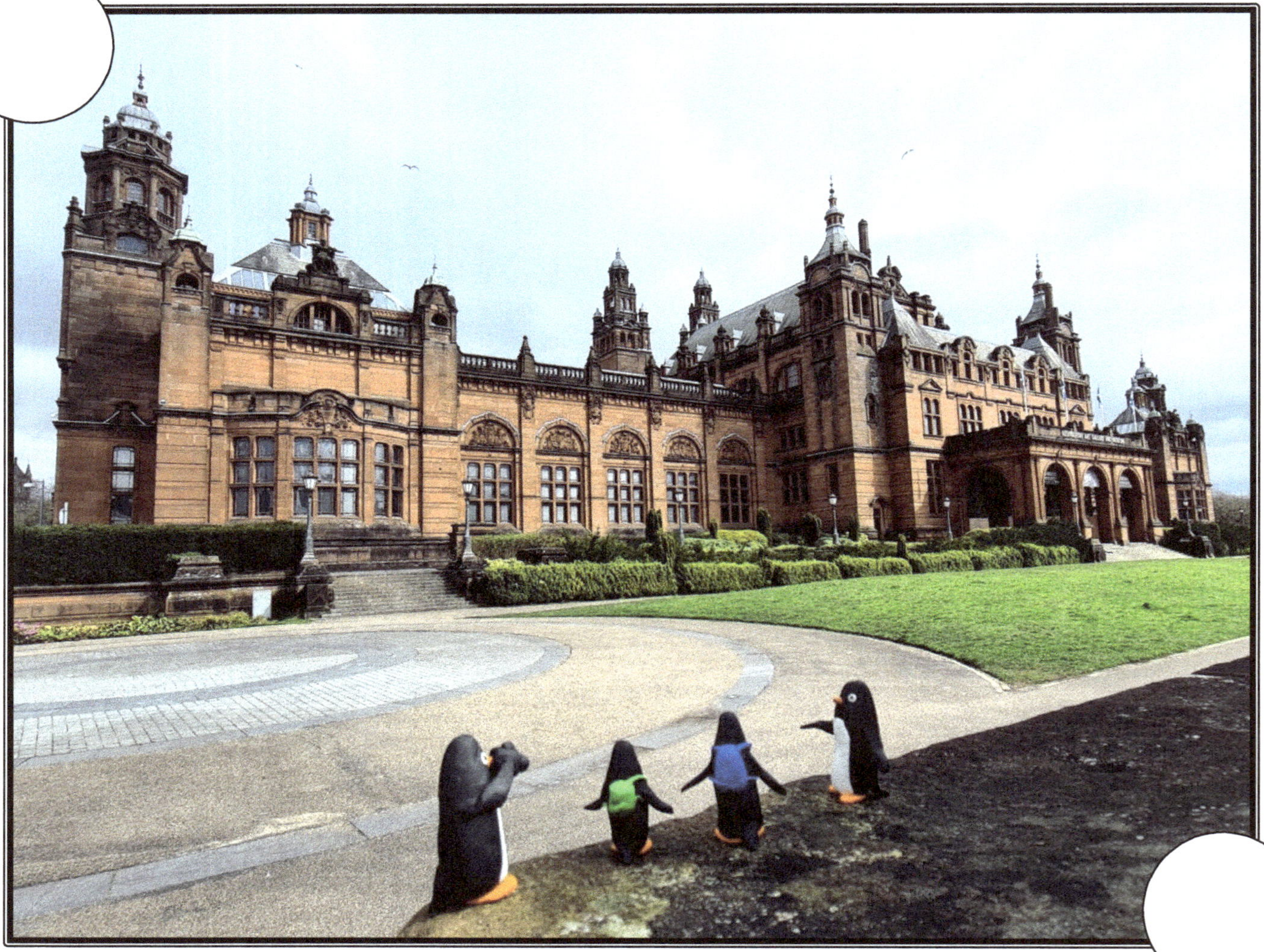

17th May 2023

Glasgow has some beautiful buildings, but this is one of my favourites. It's the Kelvingrove Art Gallery and Museum and it looks fantastic! It's also brilliant inside, and me and my Little Brother like to play hide-and-seek amongst all the amazing stuff they have in there.

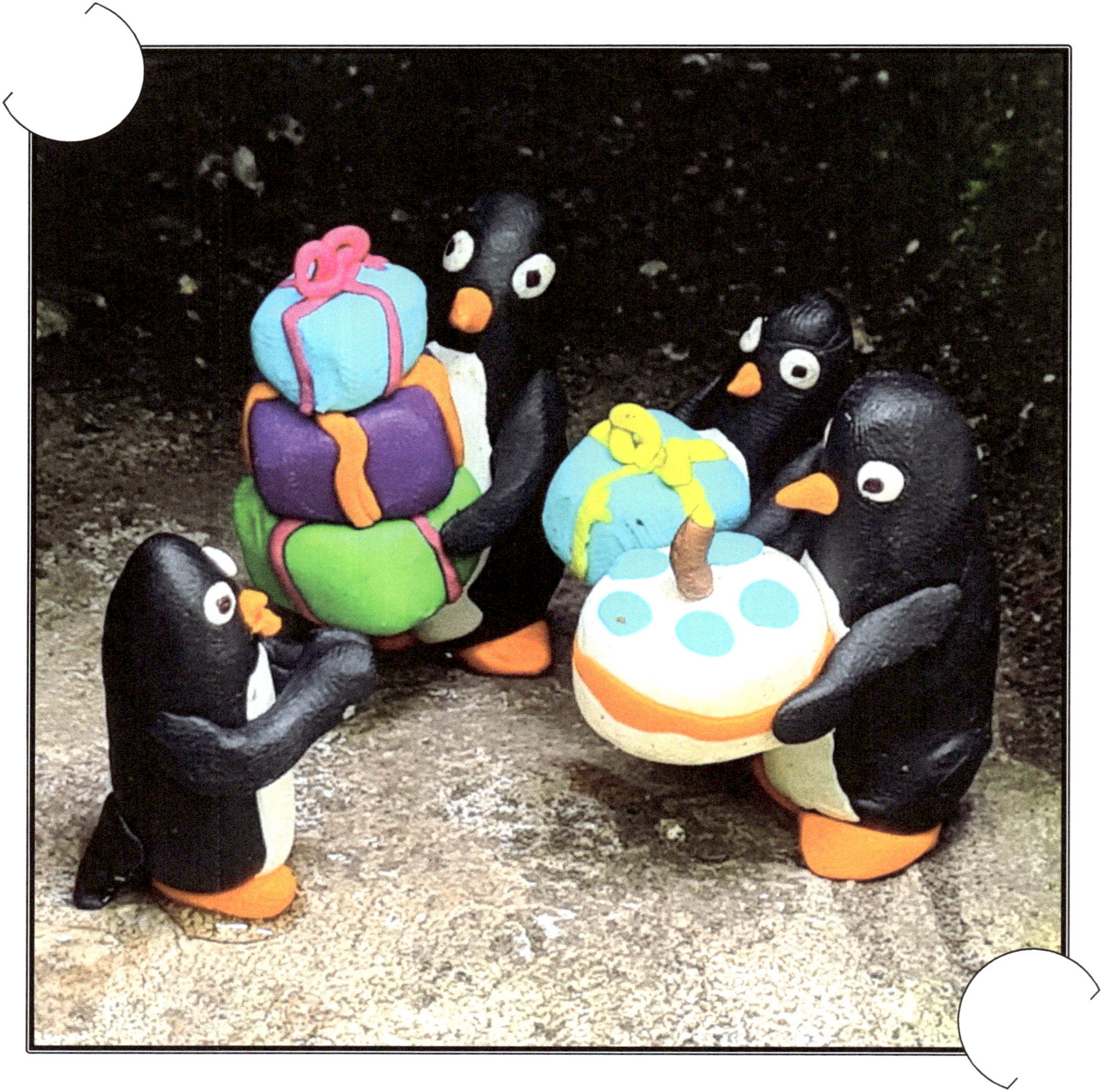

22nd May 2023

It's my Little Brother's hatchday (what you humans would call a birthday), so Mum made him a cake and we got him lots of presents.

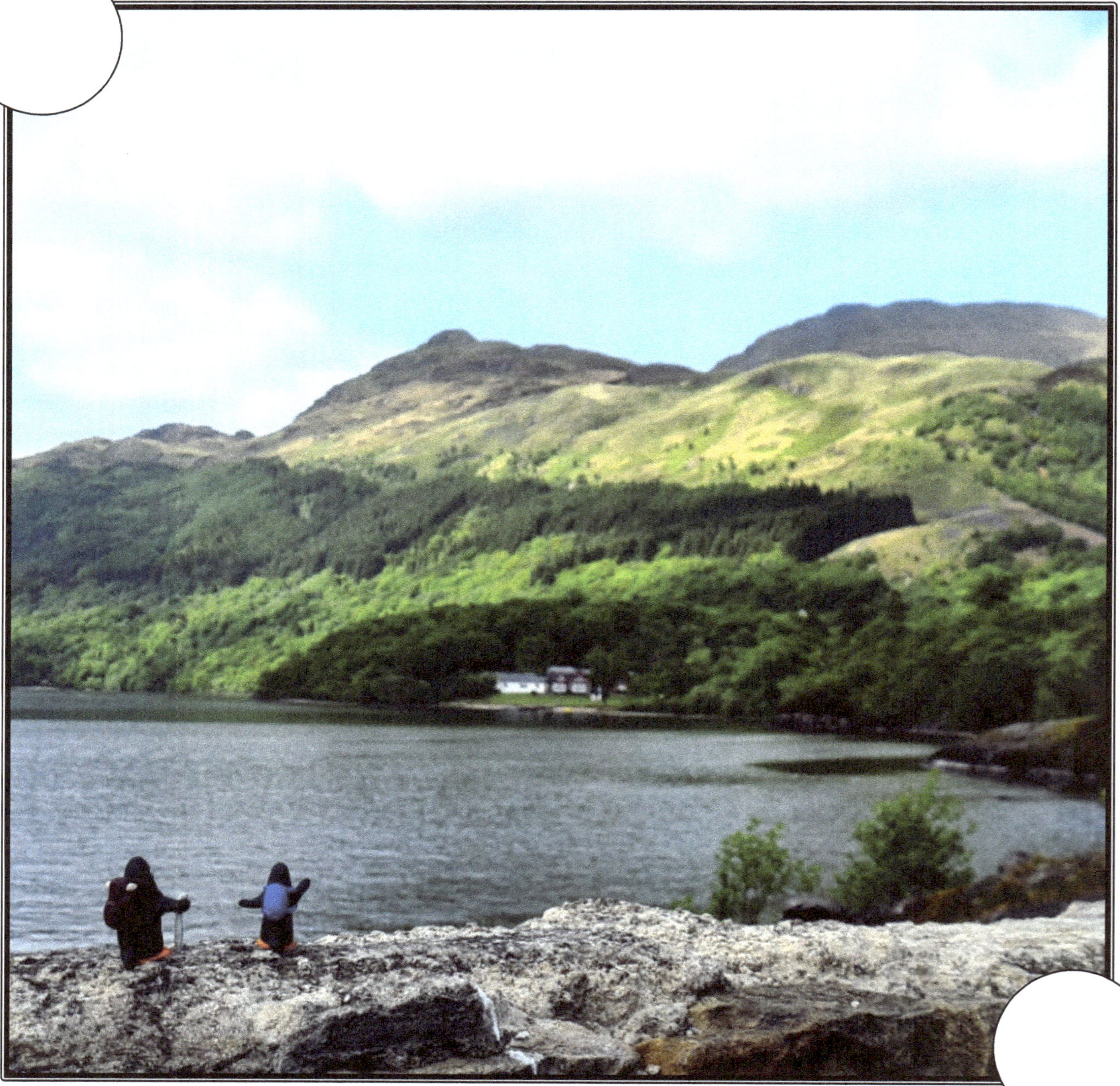

26th May 2026

I've always wanted to climb a mountain, so today me and Dad set off to climb Ben Lomond. It's the nearest mountain to where we live in Glasgow. This is us leaving from the car park at the bottom.

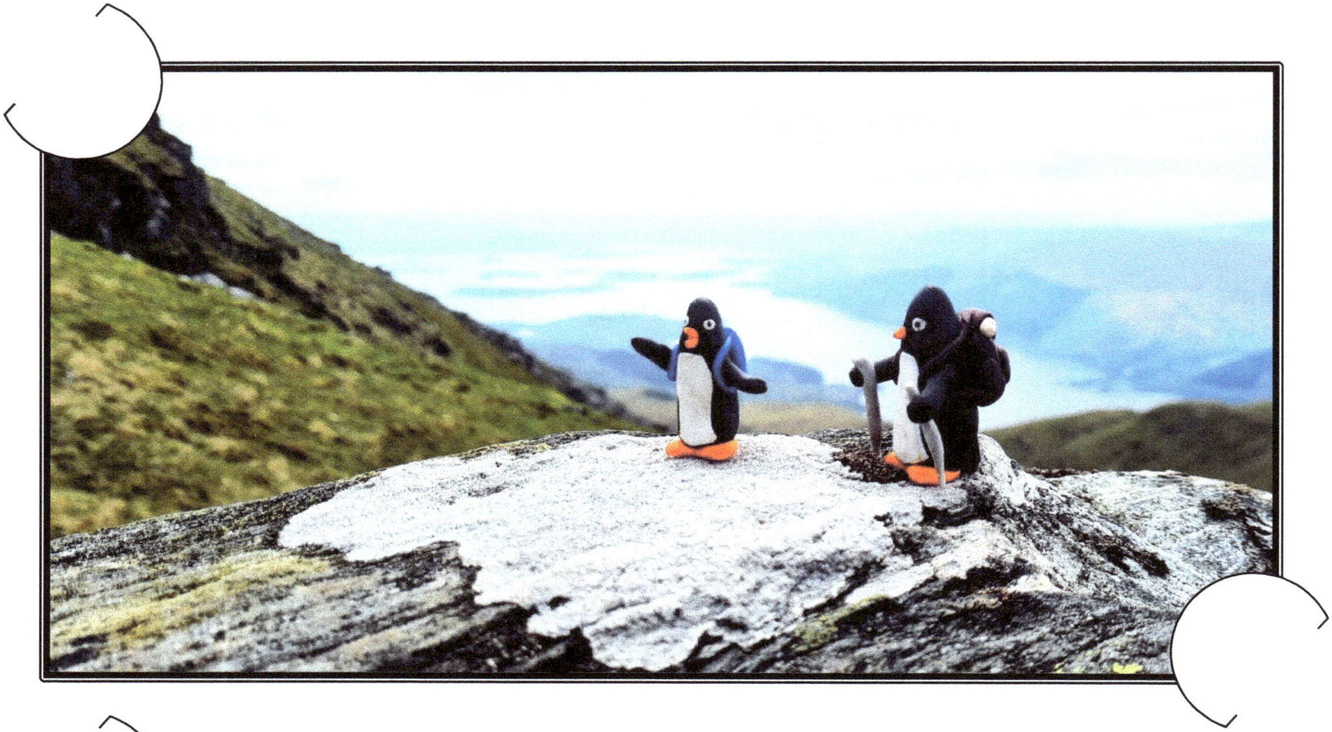

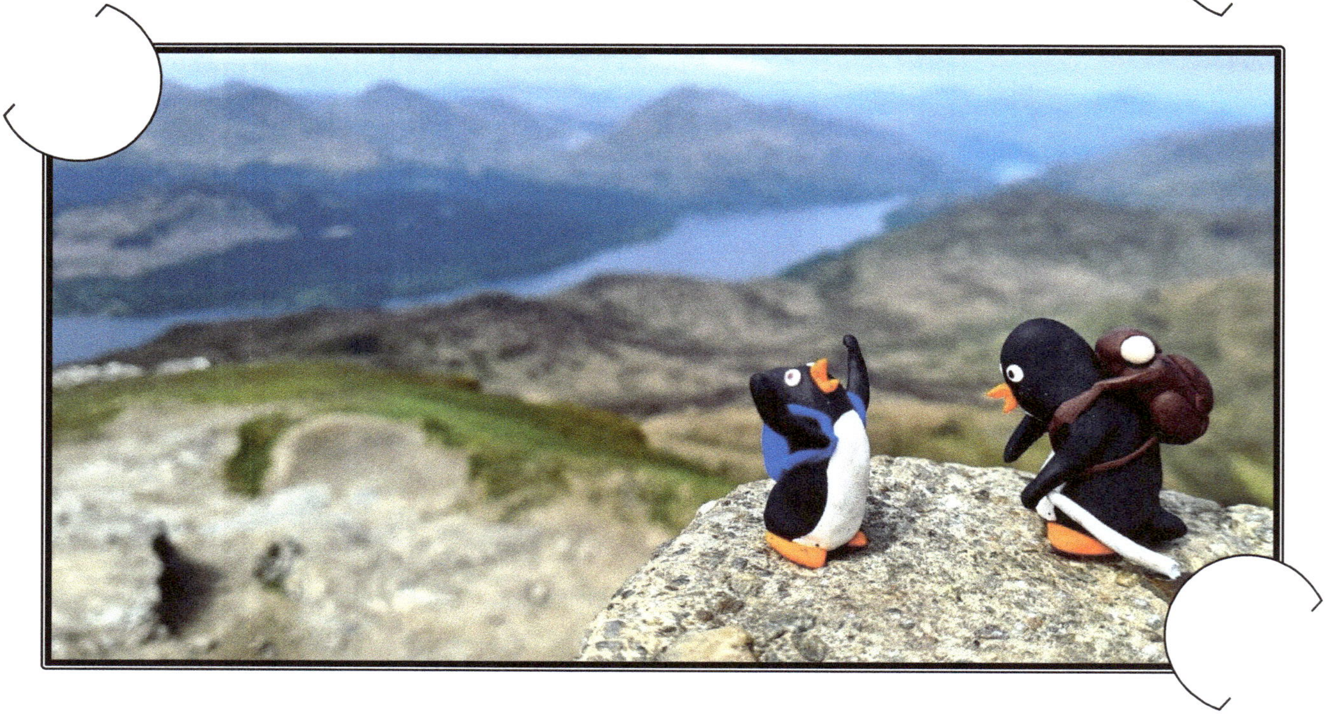

26th May 2023

These photos are of us on the mountain.
In the top photo, we're about half way up.
The views were amazing! That's Loch
Lomond in the background.

The bottom photograph is us reaching
the top of our first mountain! I really want to
do another one tomorrow, but Dad says he'll
need a long time to recover from
doing this one, a very
long time!

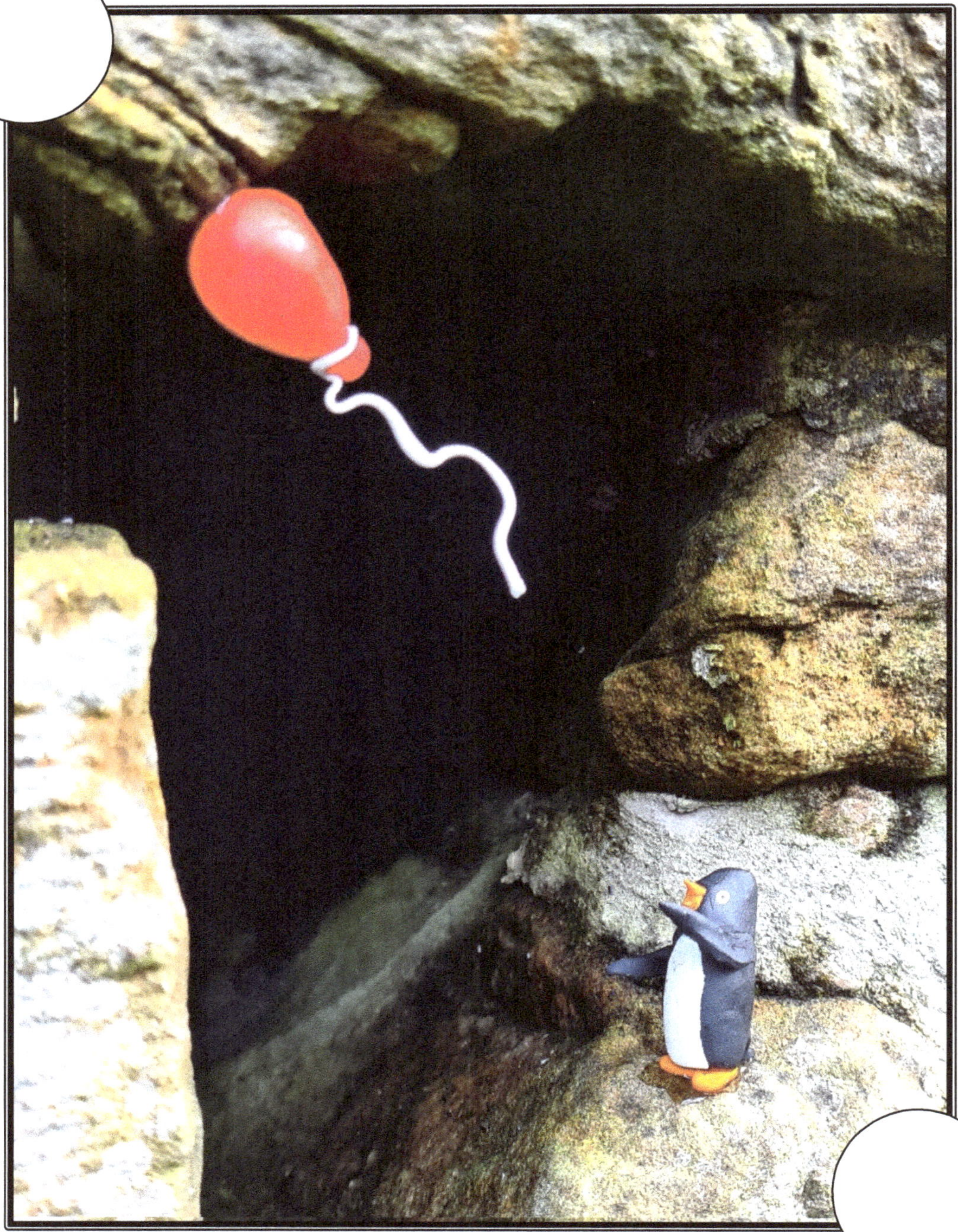

2nd June 2023

I won a big red balloon at school today for a report I wrote about my favourite artist. He's called Bansky, and he does street art, but no one knows who he is. Unfortunately, on the way home, I accidentally let it go and it floated away. I miss my balloon!!!

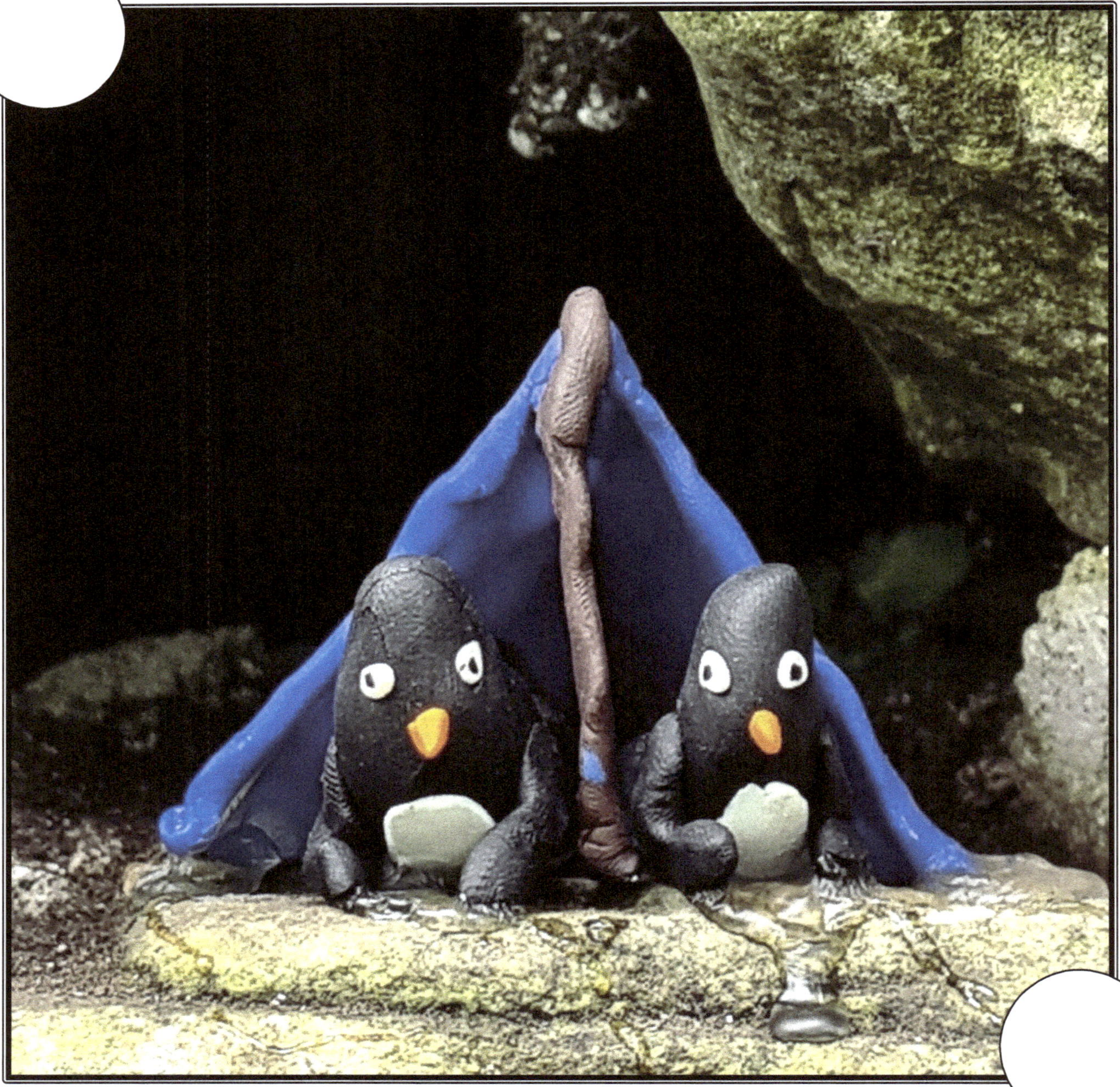

12th June 2023

My Little Brother got a tent for his hatchday, and today Mum and Dad let us sleep out in it. It was brilliant!!

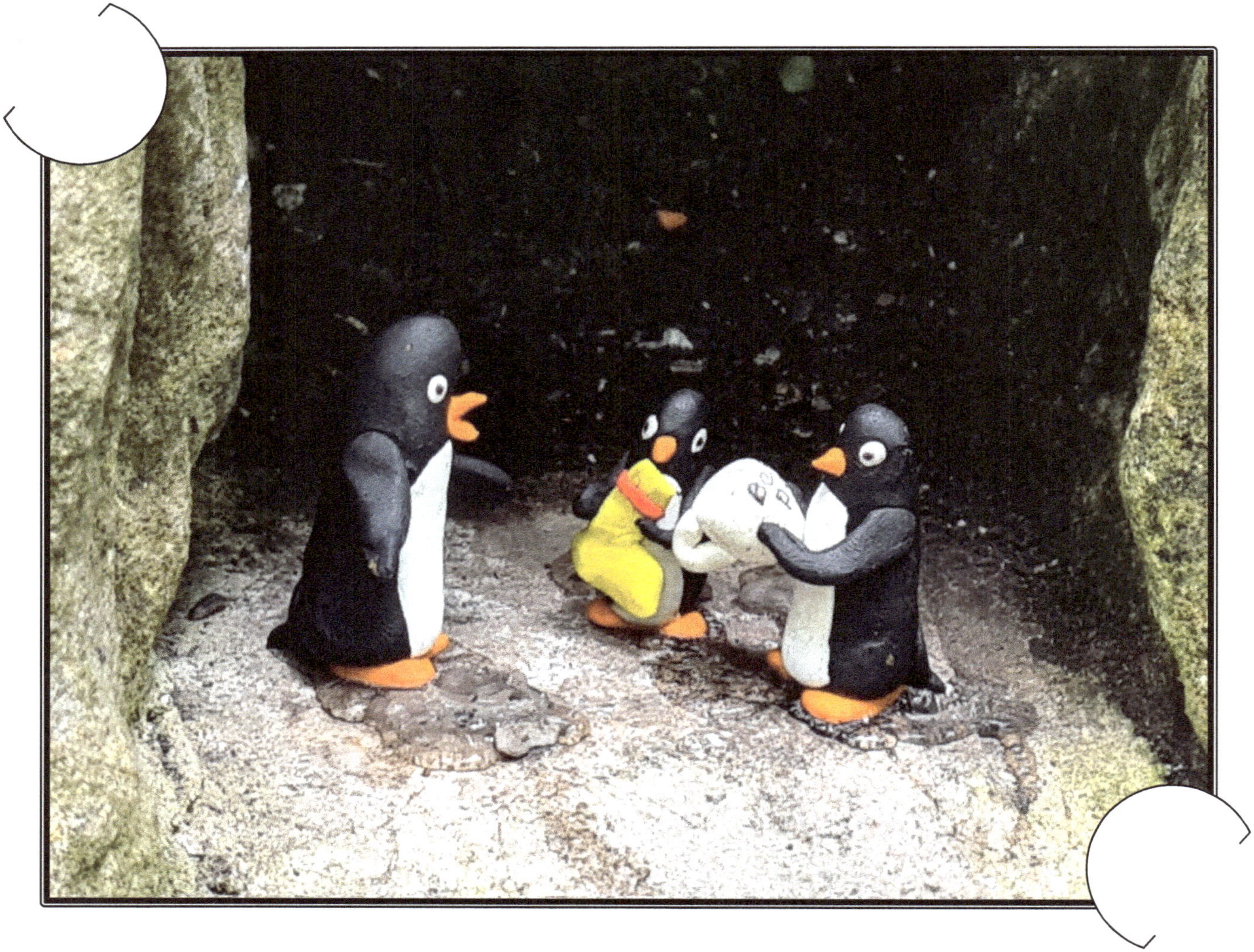

18th June 2023

As it's Father's Day, we gave Dad
some presents. I made him a mug and my
Little Brother knitted him a sock (yes, just
the one!). He said he loved both
of his presents, but I'm sure
he liked mine better!

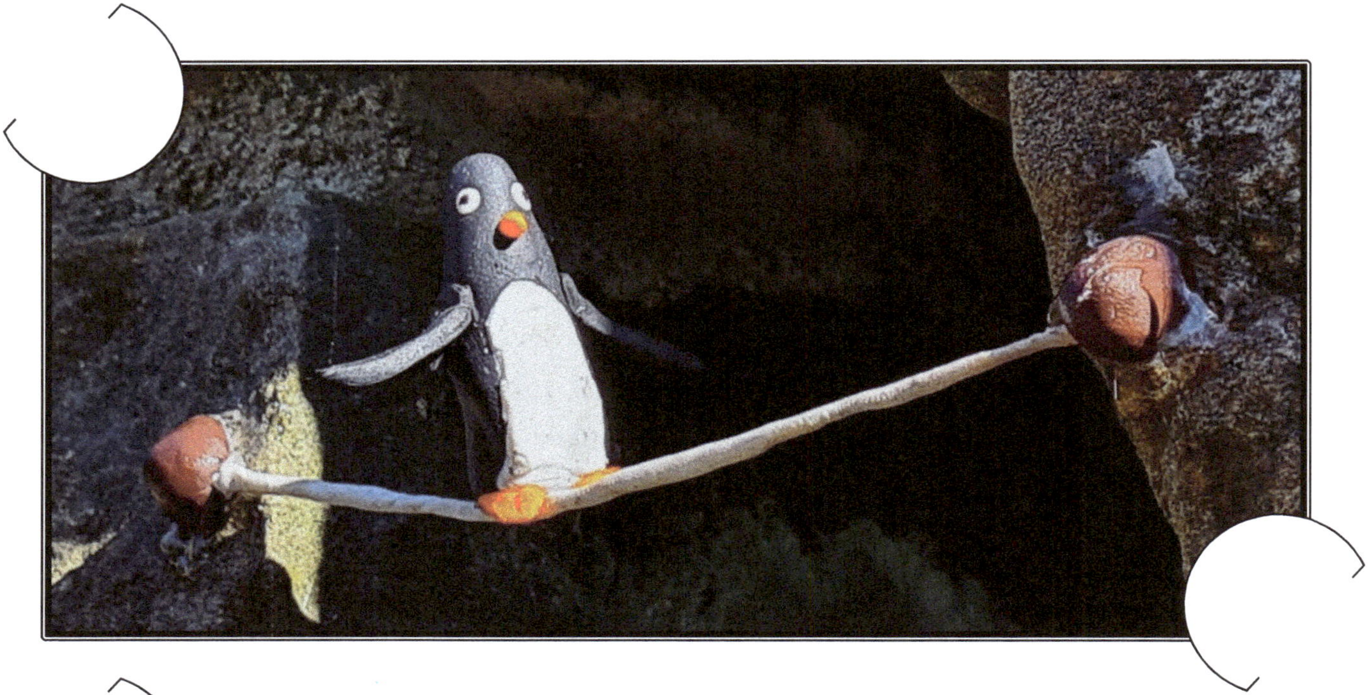

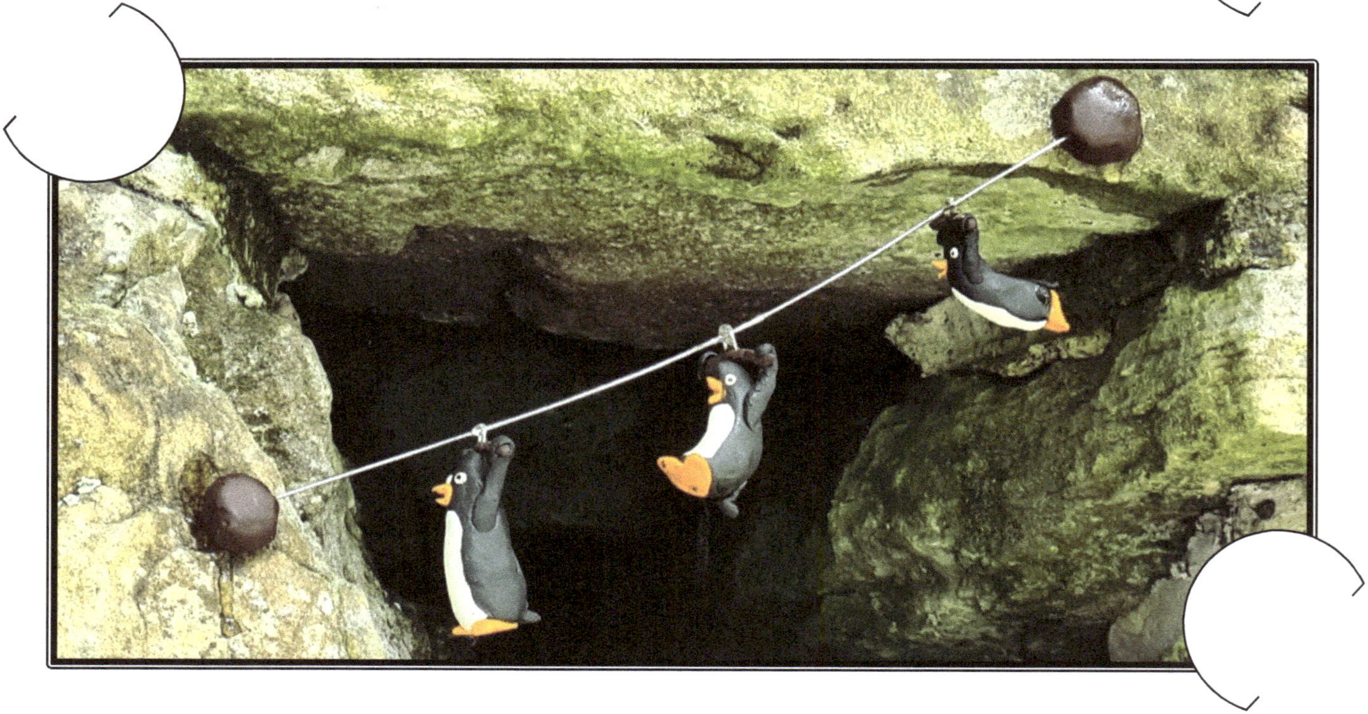

27th June 2023

Mum always likes to try new things,
and she's becoming quite the adrenaline junkie.
This is her walking on a tightrope.

Me, Dad and my Little Brother were too
scared to try it, so we went on a zip wire instead.
It was so much fun!

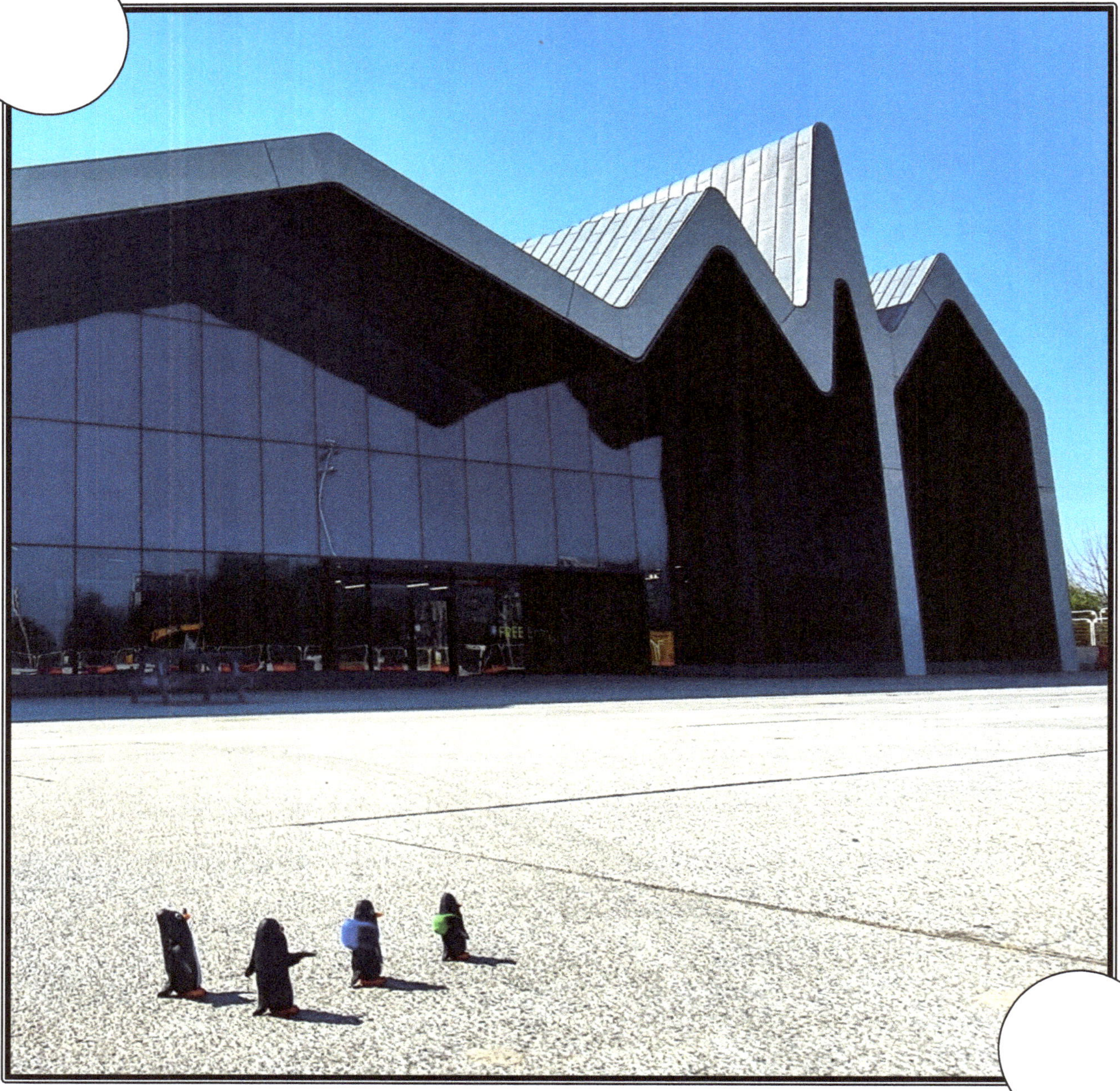
FREE

1st July 2023

Glasgow has a lot of museums, and most of them are free to visit! This is the Riverside Museum, and its got all sorts of buses and trains and ships inside it. We always have a lot of fun when we go there!

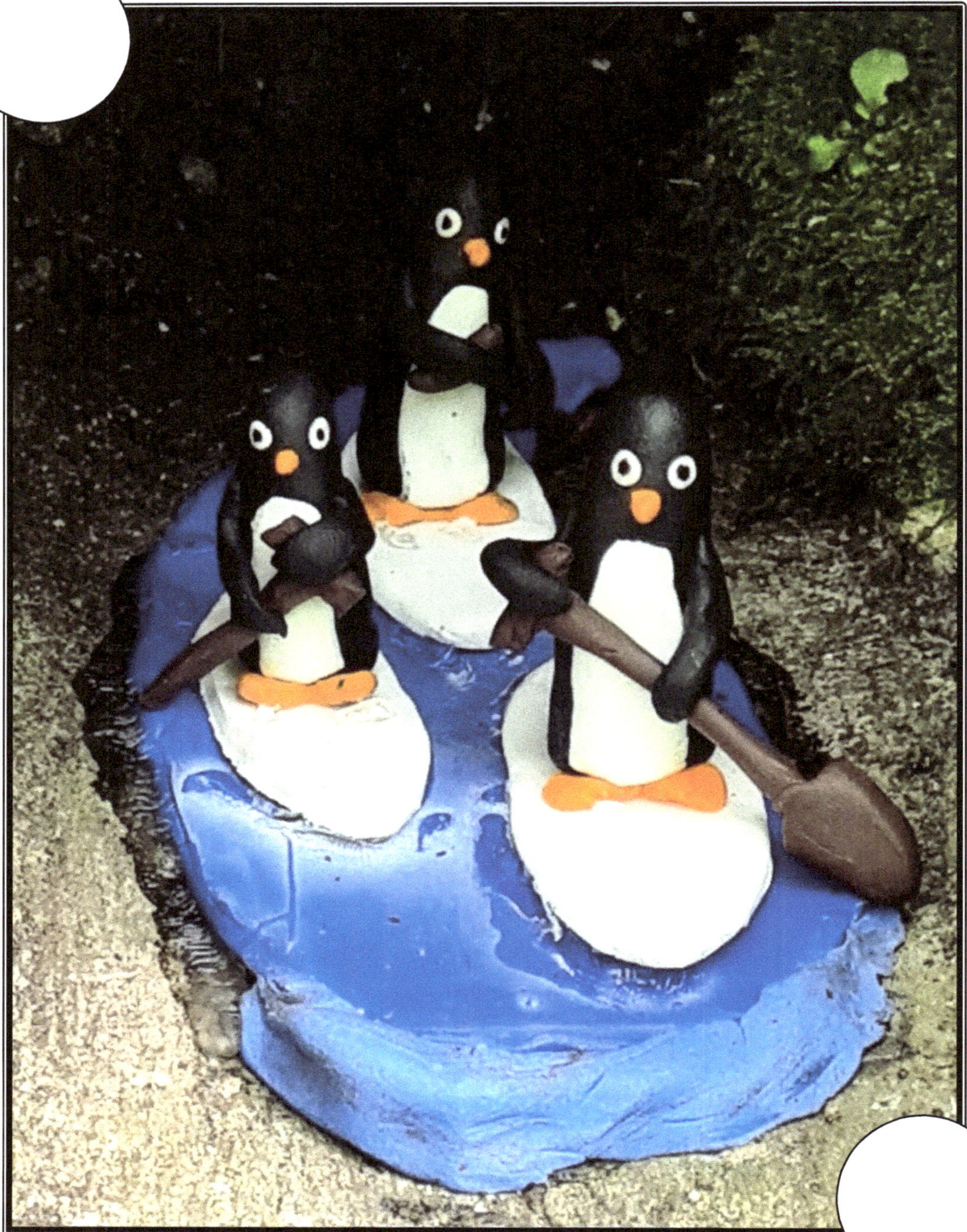

5th July 2023

As it's the school holidays, we get to go on lots of adventures. Today, Mum took us paddleboarding. I loved it, but it was very tiring.

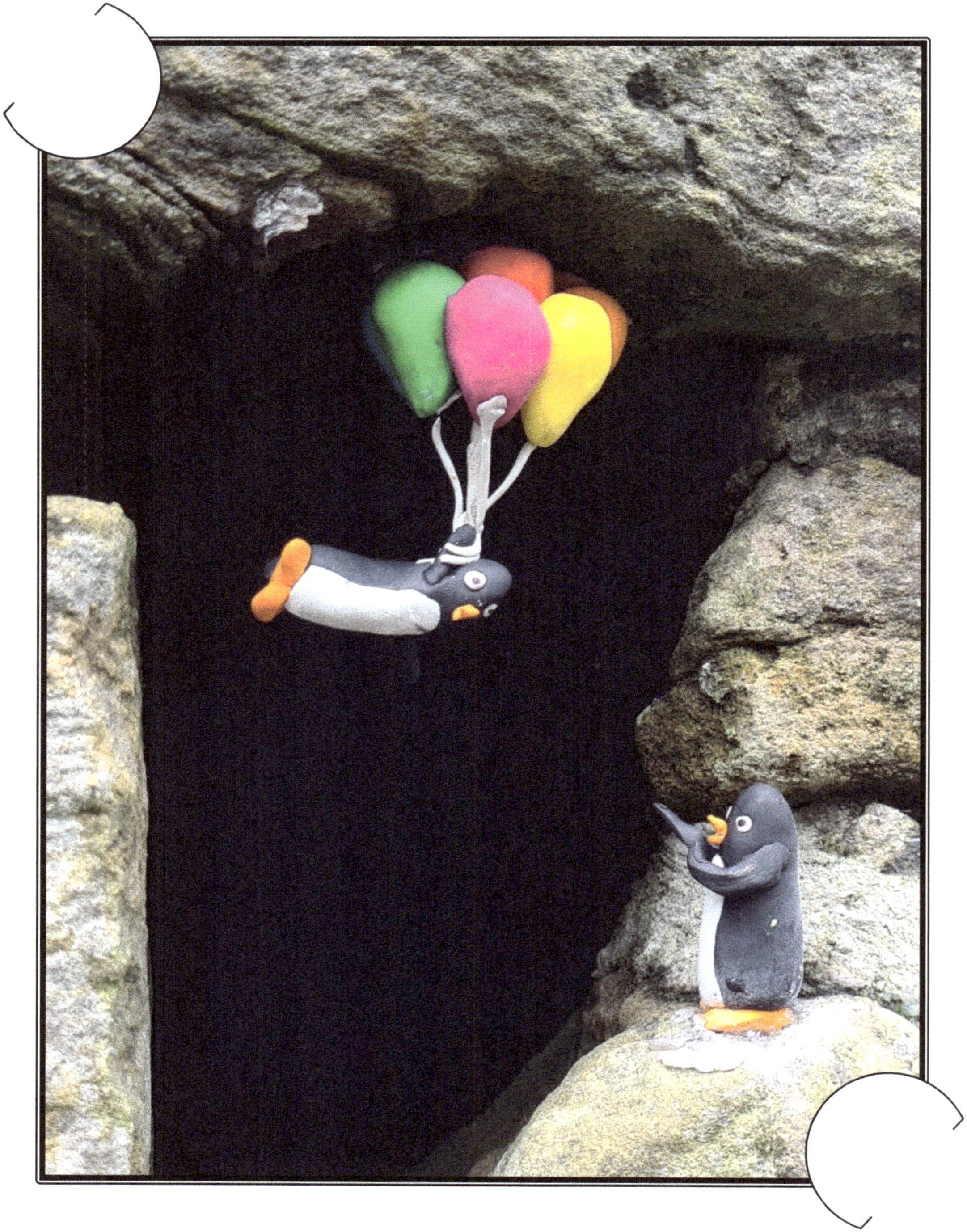

8th July 2023

Dad was looking after us today, and he told my Little Brother that if he tidied his room, he'd buy him some balloons. I told Dad he'd gotten too many, but he never listens to me. Don't worry, he came down eventually. Mum says Dad's not allowed to babysit my Little Brother on his own again for a very long time!

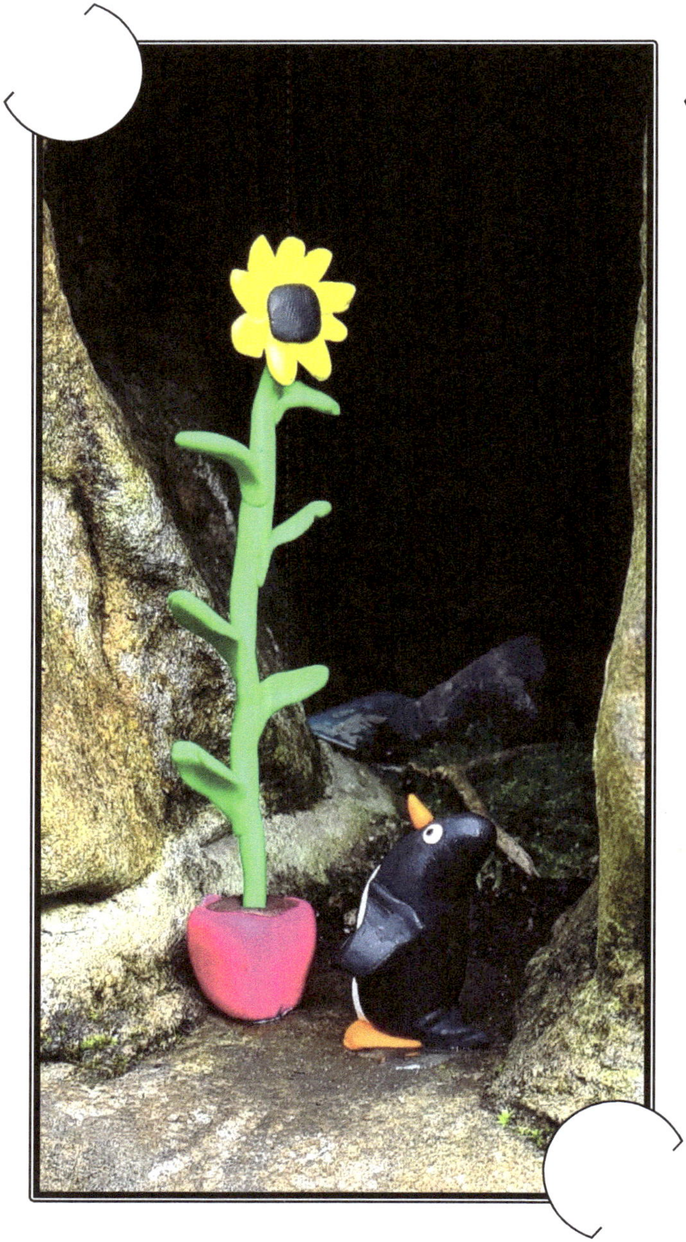
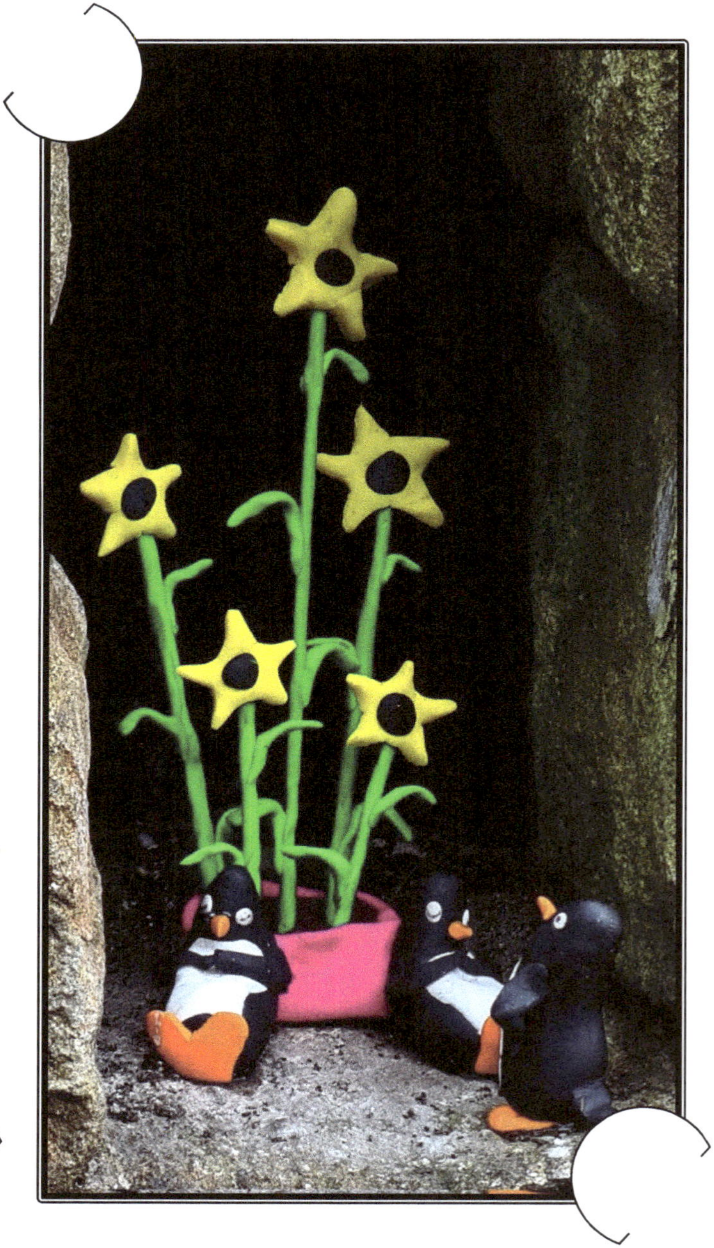

13th July 2023

As well as doing extreme sports,
Mum likes to grow things in our garden.
These are some sunflowers she grew. They're
absolutely massive, but they're a nice shady
place to fall asleep when the sun's out!

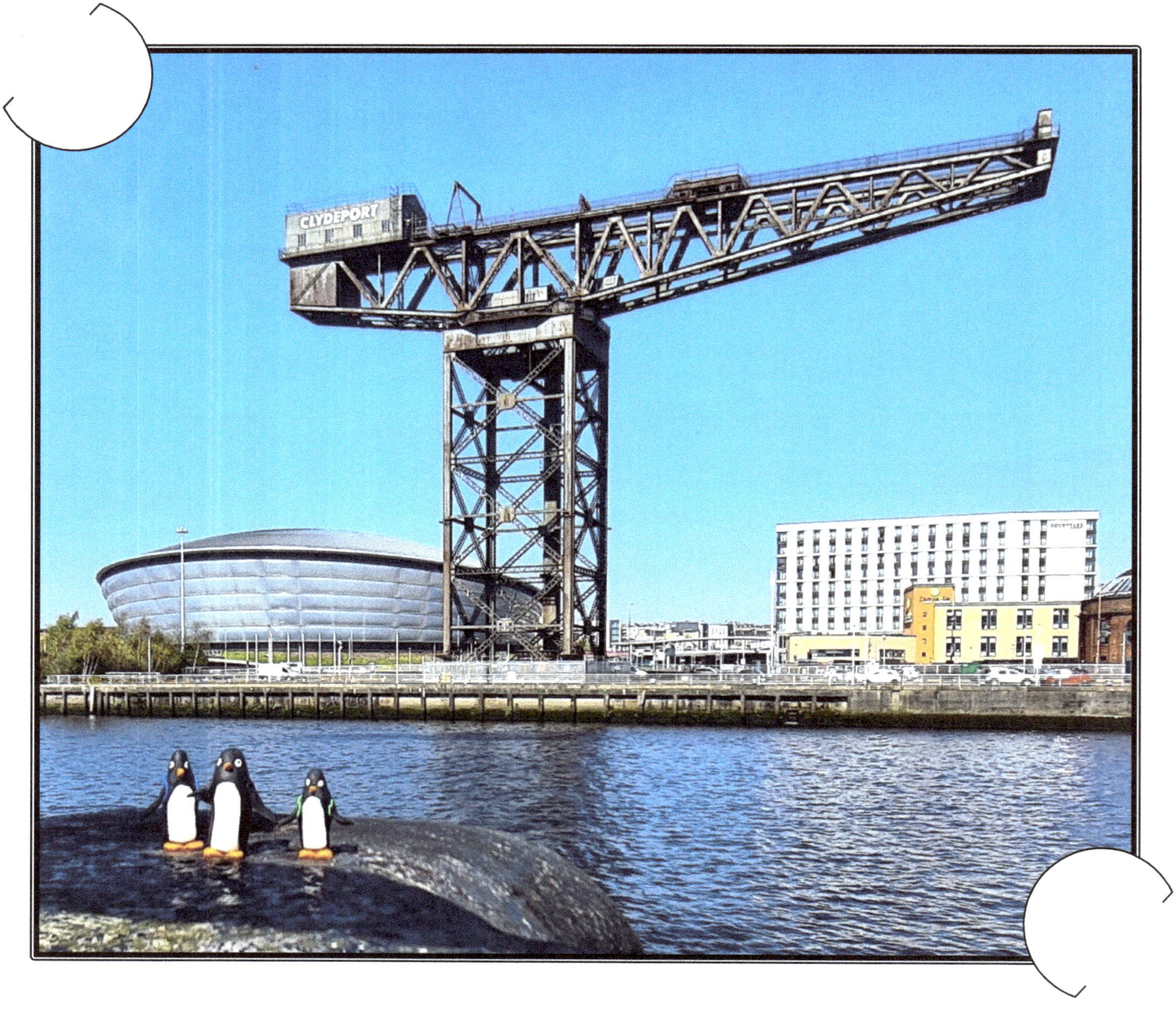
CLYDEPORT

26th July 2023

The Clyde is much larger than the river by our wall, and it runs right through the middle of Glasgow. There's this massive old crane beside it that looks nothing else I've ever seen. Mum says it would make a great spot to do a bungee jump. Dad says she's out of her mind!

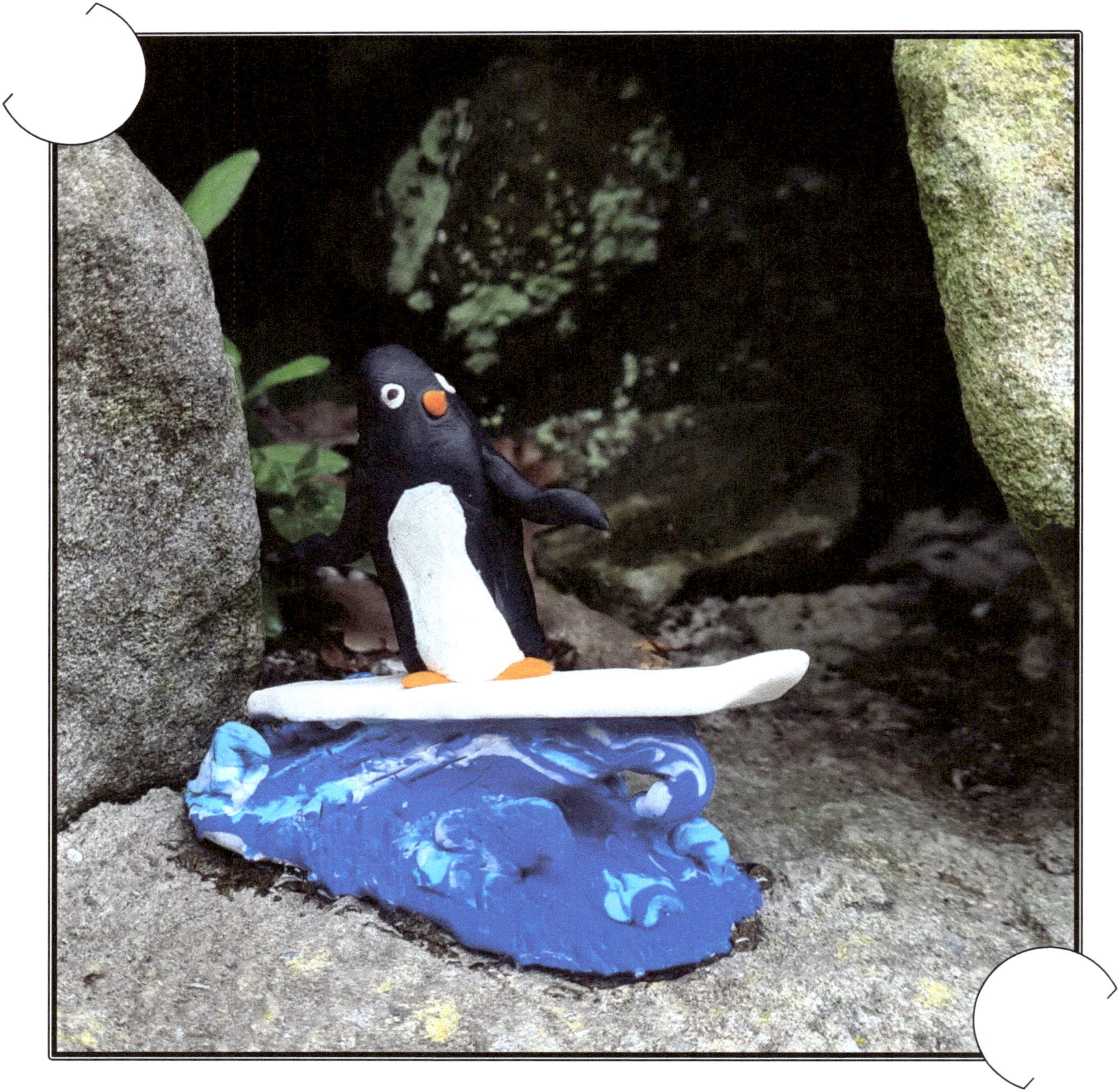

2nd August 2023

As well as paddleboarding, Mum really likes to go surfing. She says it's so much fun and that she'll teach me how to do it once I'm a bit older.

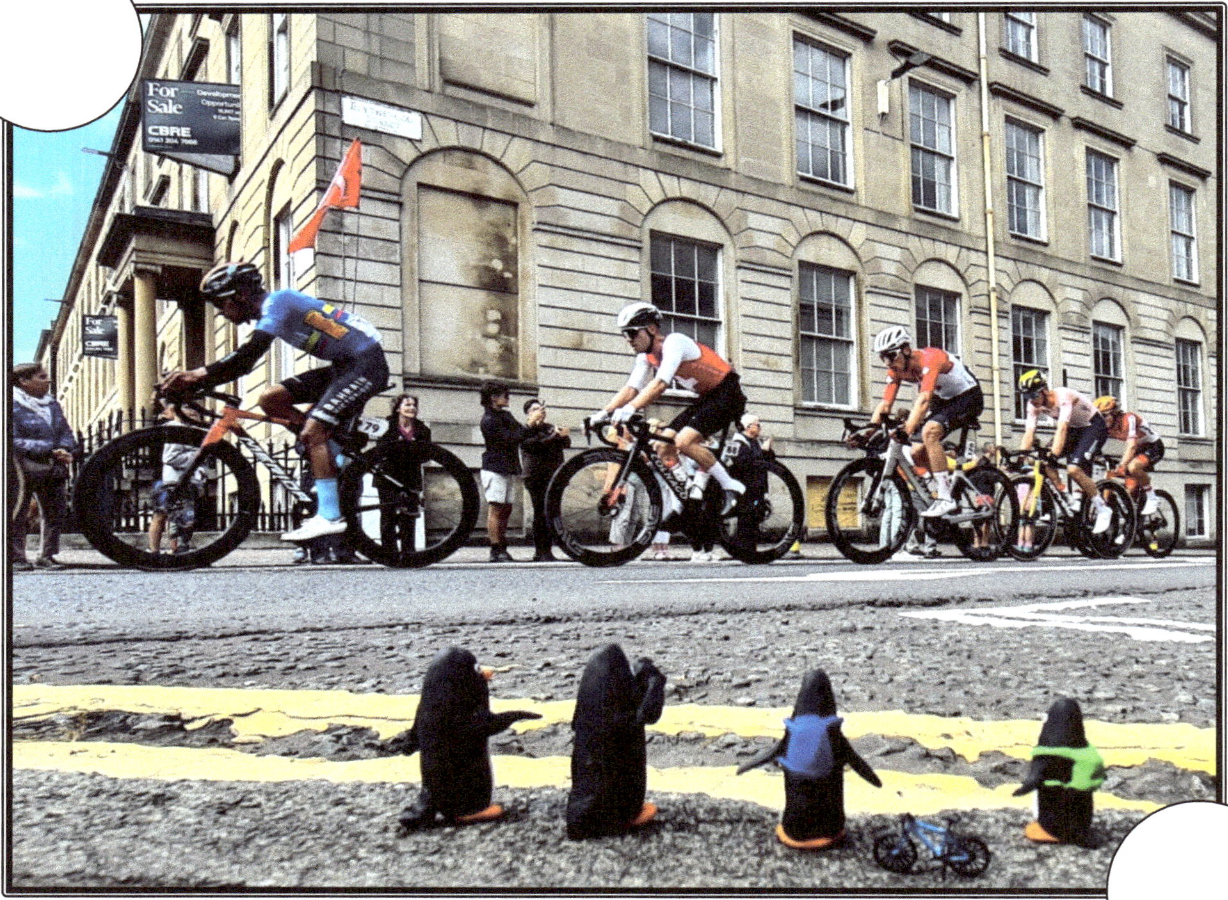
For Sale
CBRE

6th August 2023

The Cycling World Championships are in
Glasgow at the moment. It's the biggest single
cycling event ever in the history
of the world!

Today, we took a trip into Glasgow
city centre to watch the Men's Road Race.
One day, I want to be able to ride
my bike that fast!

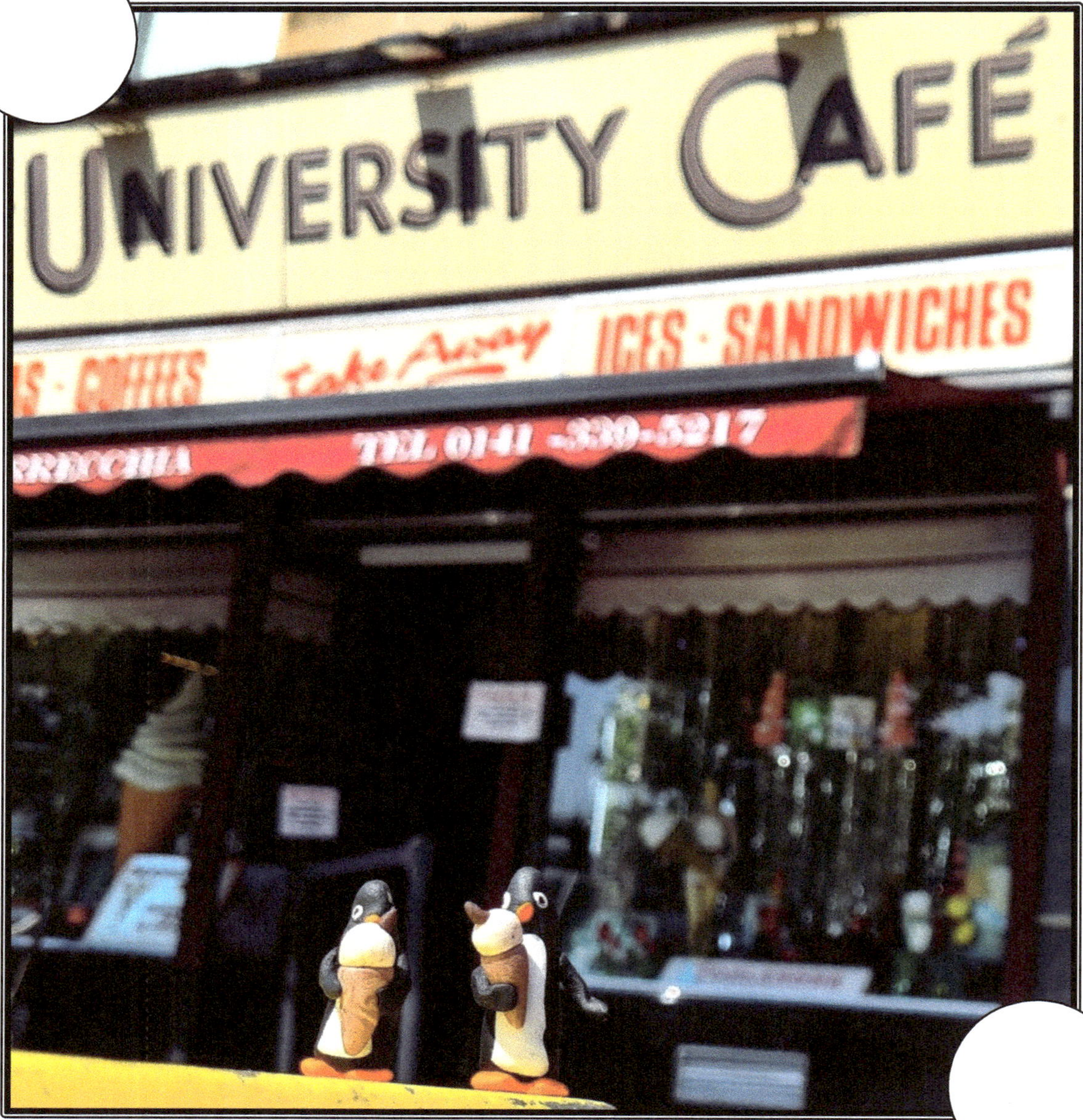
UNIVERSITY CAFÉ
Take Away
ICES · SANDWICHES
TEL 0141 339-5217

10th August 2023

Like many others who live in the West End of Glasgow, when the sun comes out and we start getting a bit too hot, we head off to the University Cafe for an ice cream.

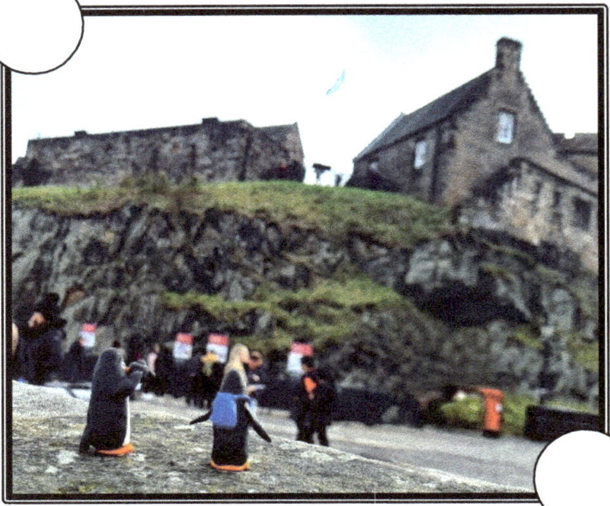

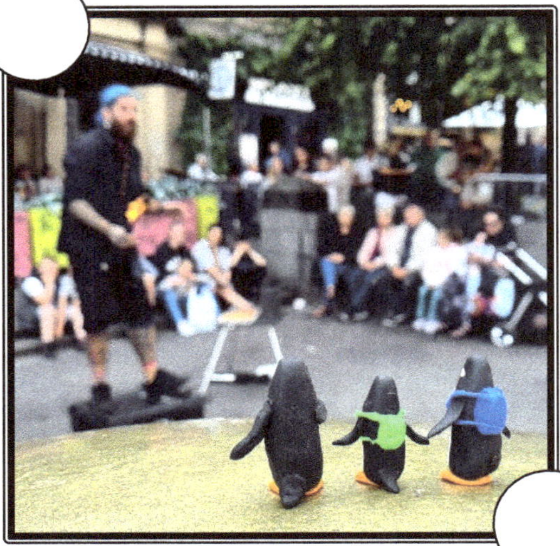

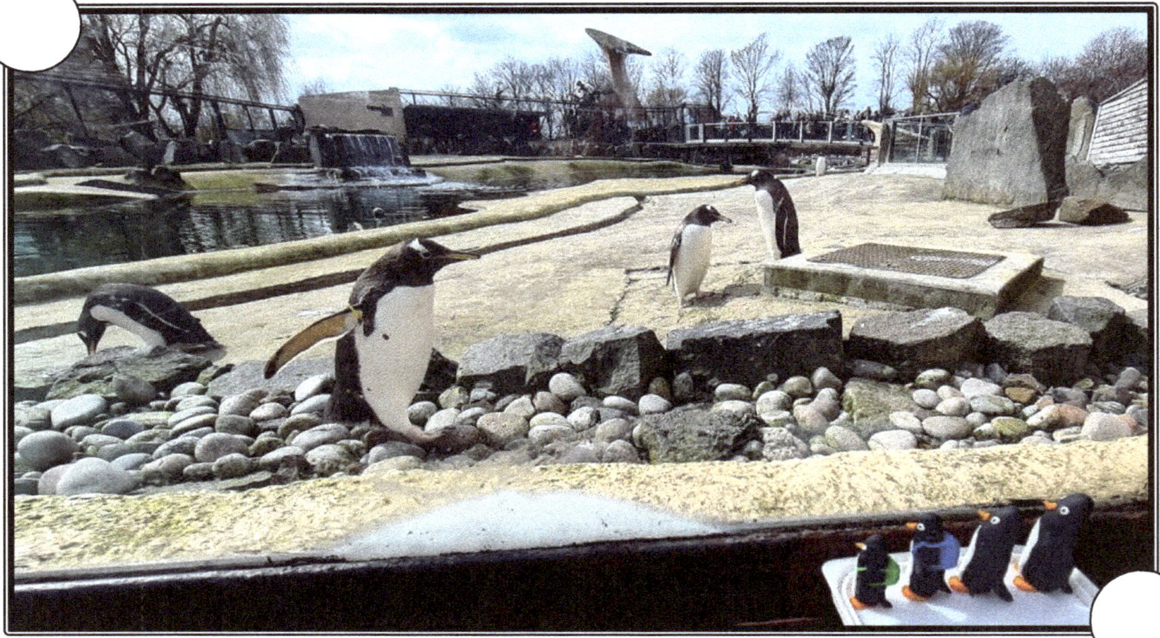

14th August 2023

Today we took a trip through to Edinburgh, which is another city in Scotland. First we went to Edinburgh Castle. It's very impressive, but there were a lot of hills and stairs for our little legs to cope with!

Then we went to the Royal Mile and watched some street performers who were there for the Fringe Festival. They were amazing. I wonder if I could learn to juggle?

Finally, we went to visit my Uncle Nils and his friends who live in Edinburgh Zoo. It was all a lot of fun, but it was also nice when we got back to Glasgow.

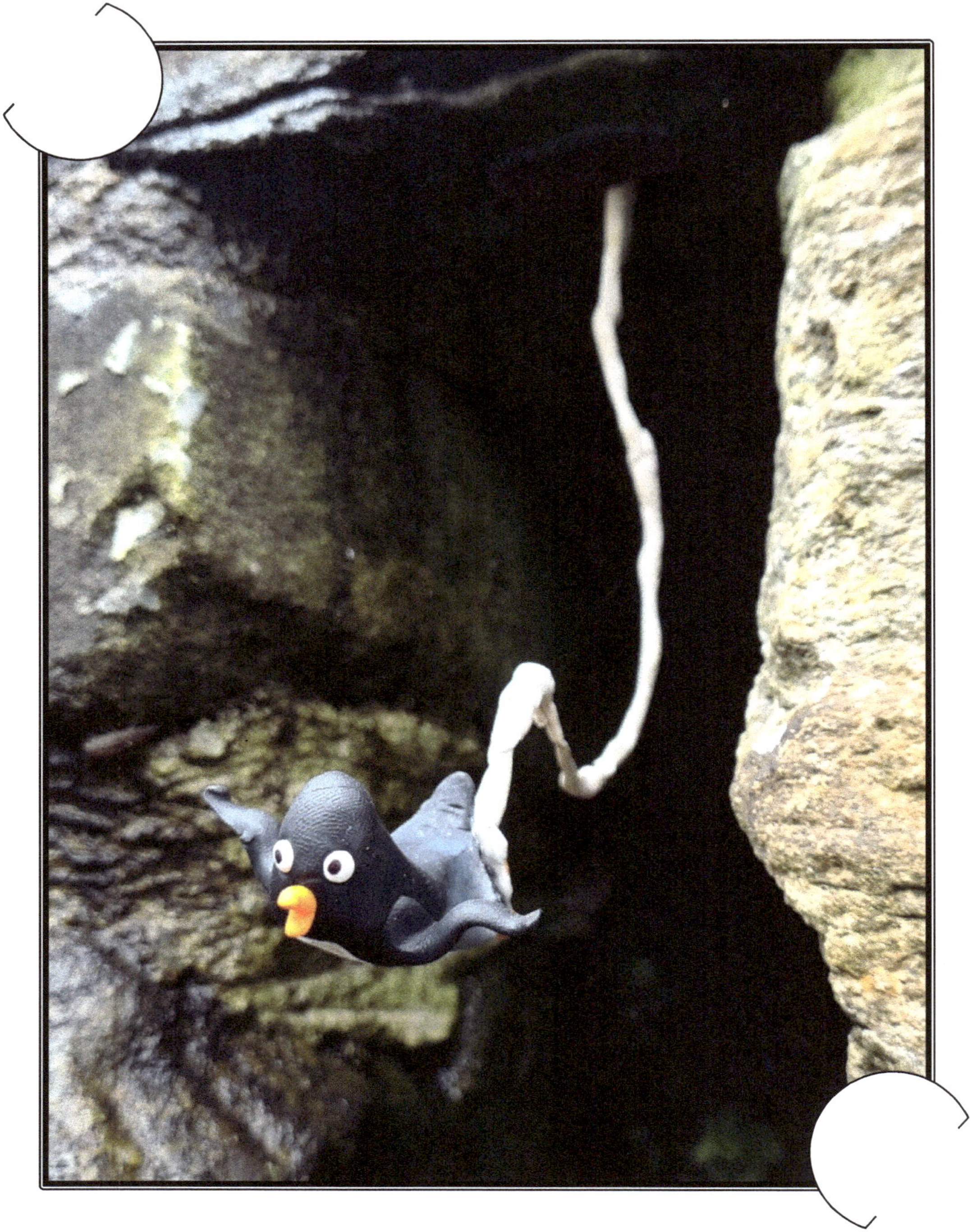

20th August 2023

Mum finally got to try bungee jumping today. She says it's about as close as a penguin can get to flying!

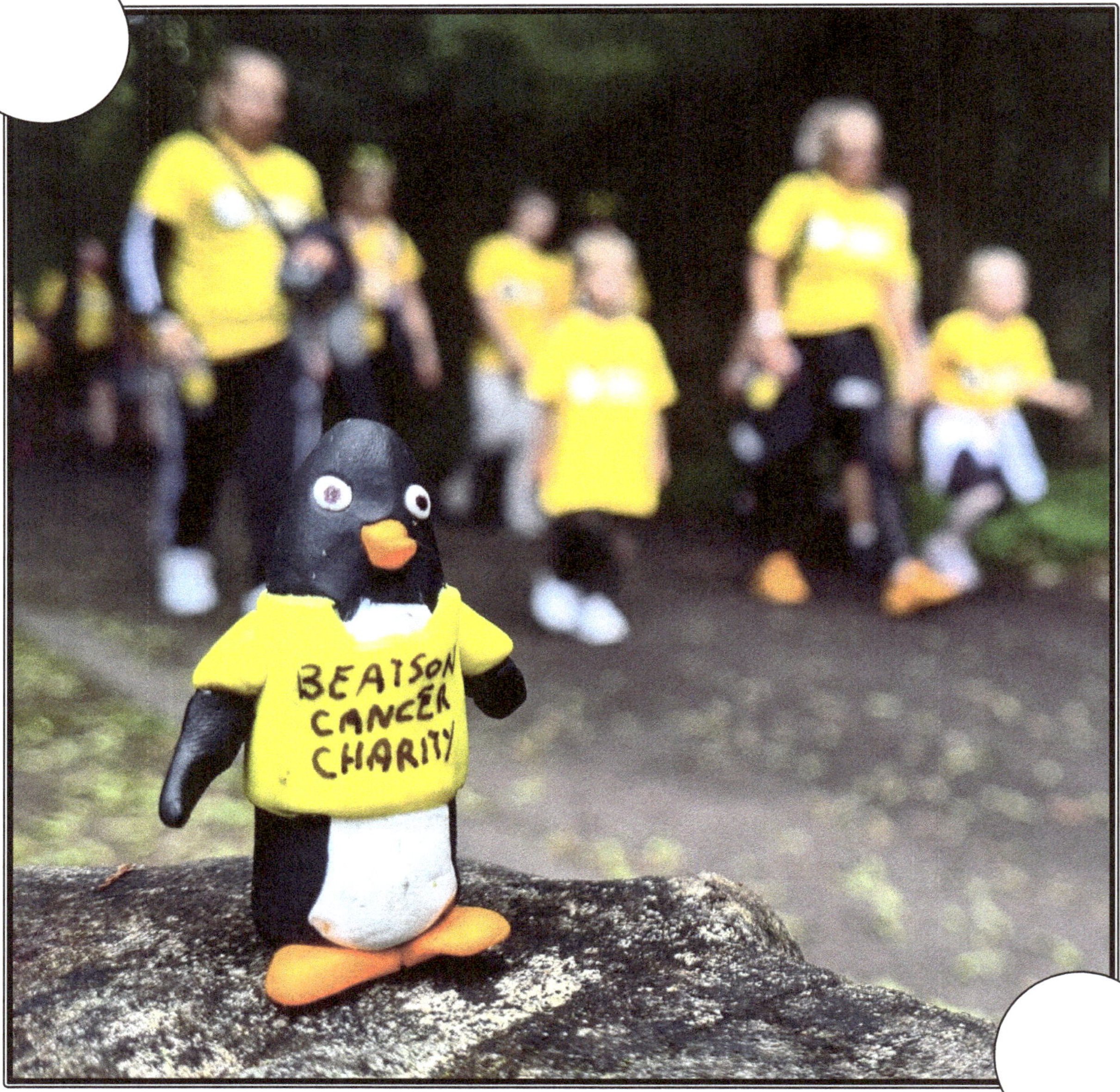
BEATSON
CANCER
CHARITY

27th August 2023

Today, the Off The Beatson Track event took place and it went right past our wall! It raises money for a very good Glasgow Charity, and loads of very nice people took part in it. Mum being Mum decided she wanted to do it too. It was ten kilometres long and she managed to waddle the whole way without stopping. We were all very proud of her.

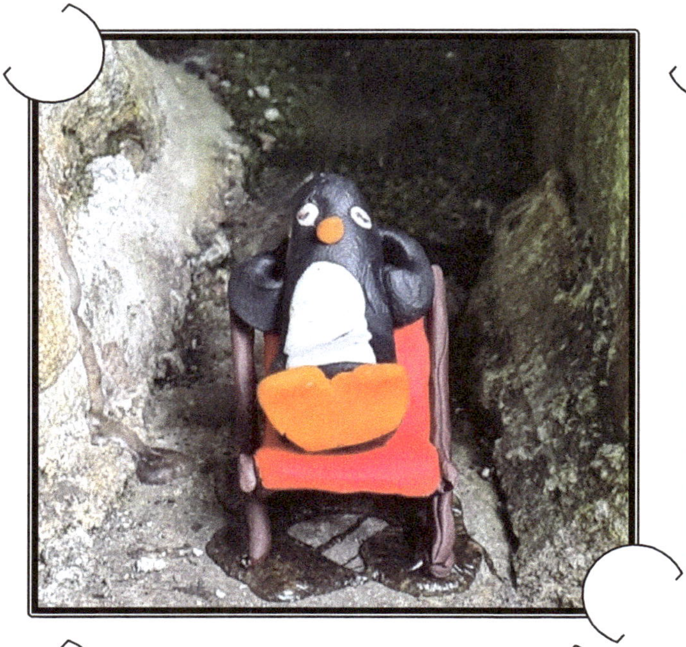
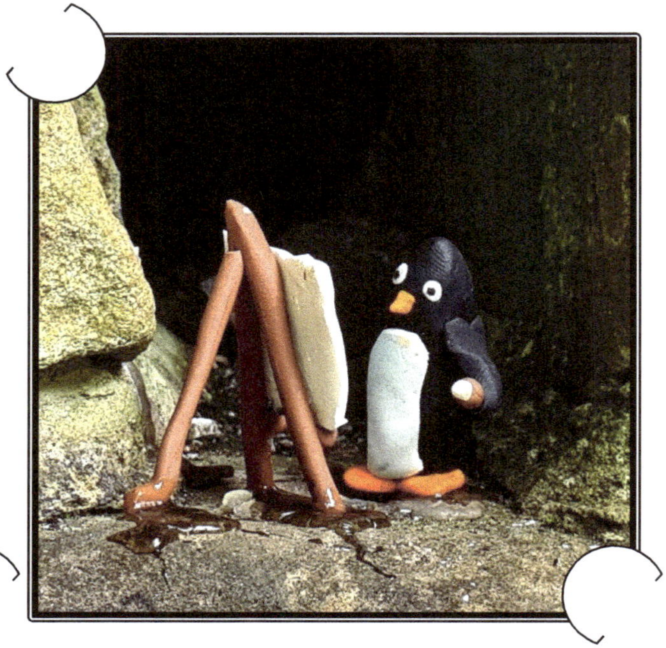
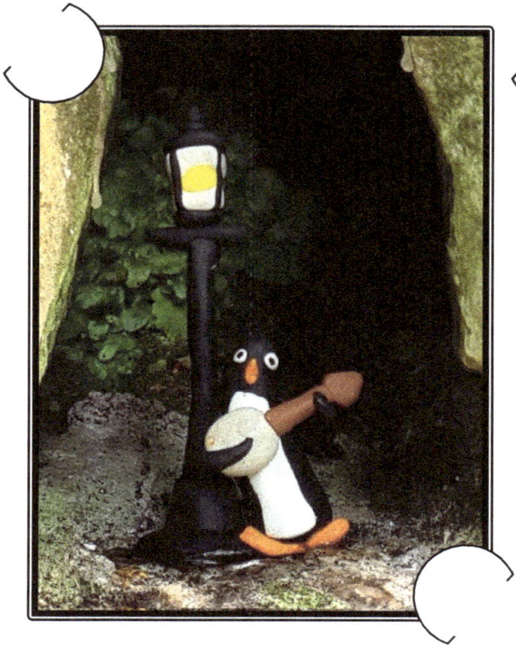
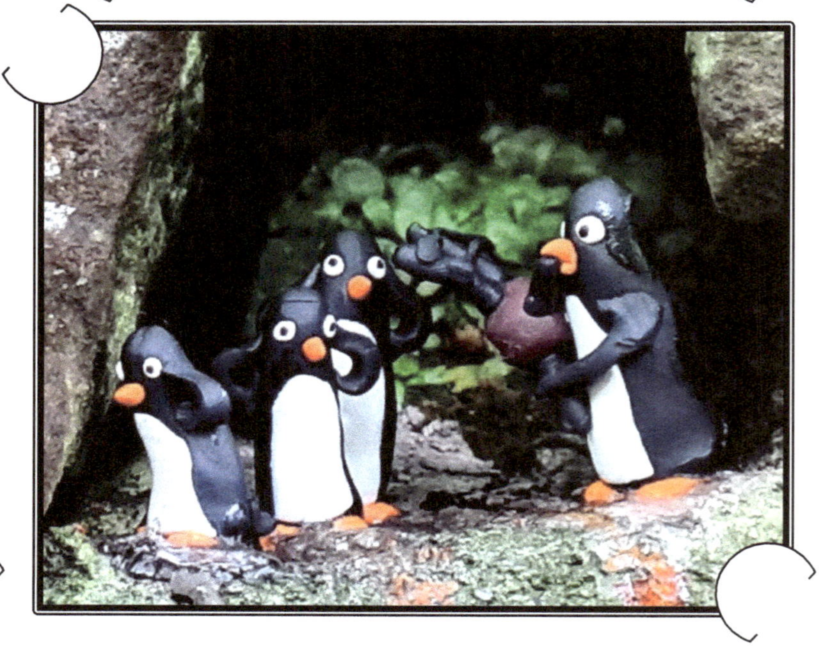

1st September 2023

Just like Mum, Dad has lots of hobbies, but his are less active. He likes sleeping in the sun, painting, and playing his ukulele. He's also trying to learn how to play the bagpipes. He enjoys it, but we don't because he's really not very good at it.

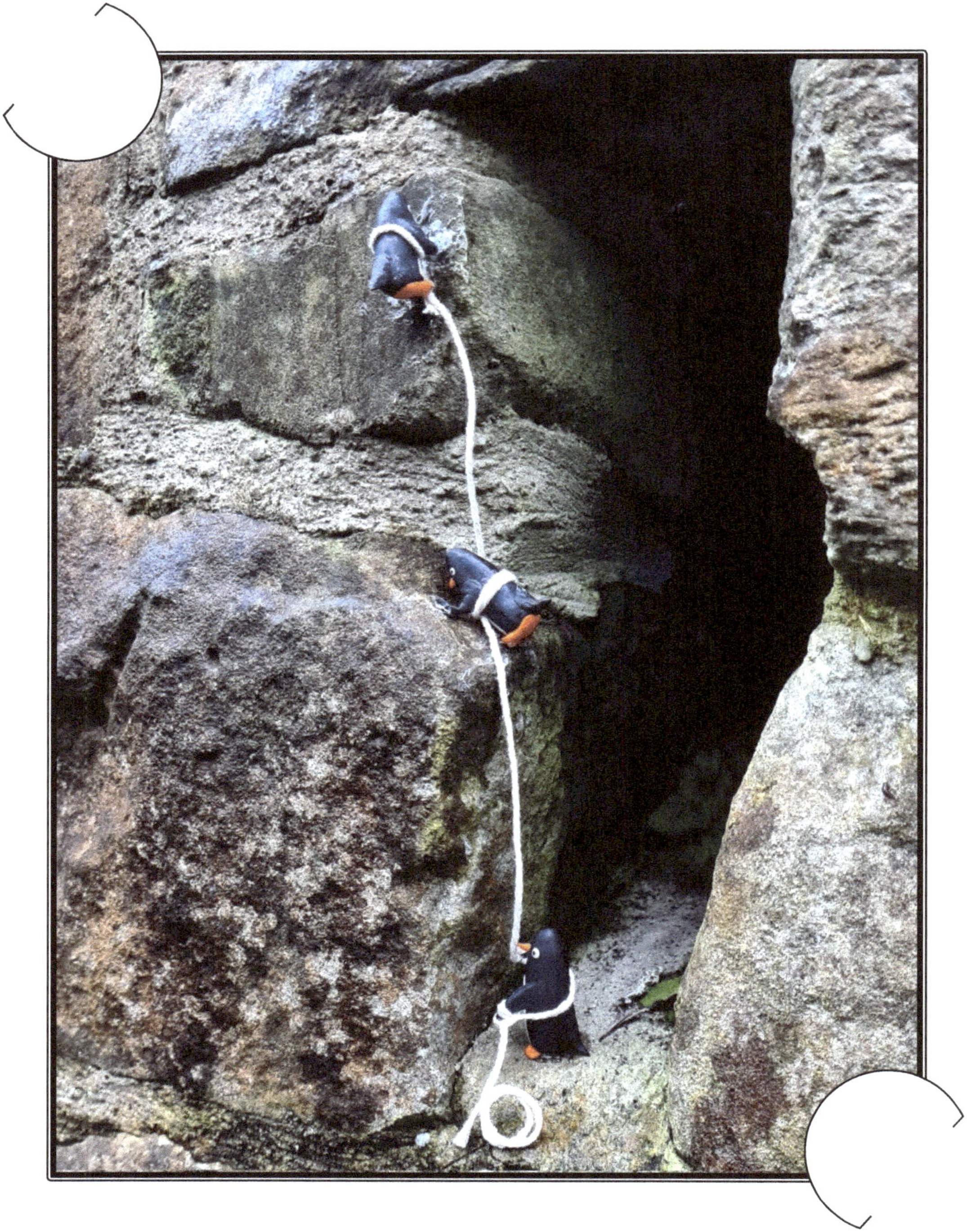

9th September 2023

Whenever Dad gets out his bagpipes,
Mum takes us off out to do something else so
we don't have to listen to him. Today, she
took us climbing.

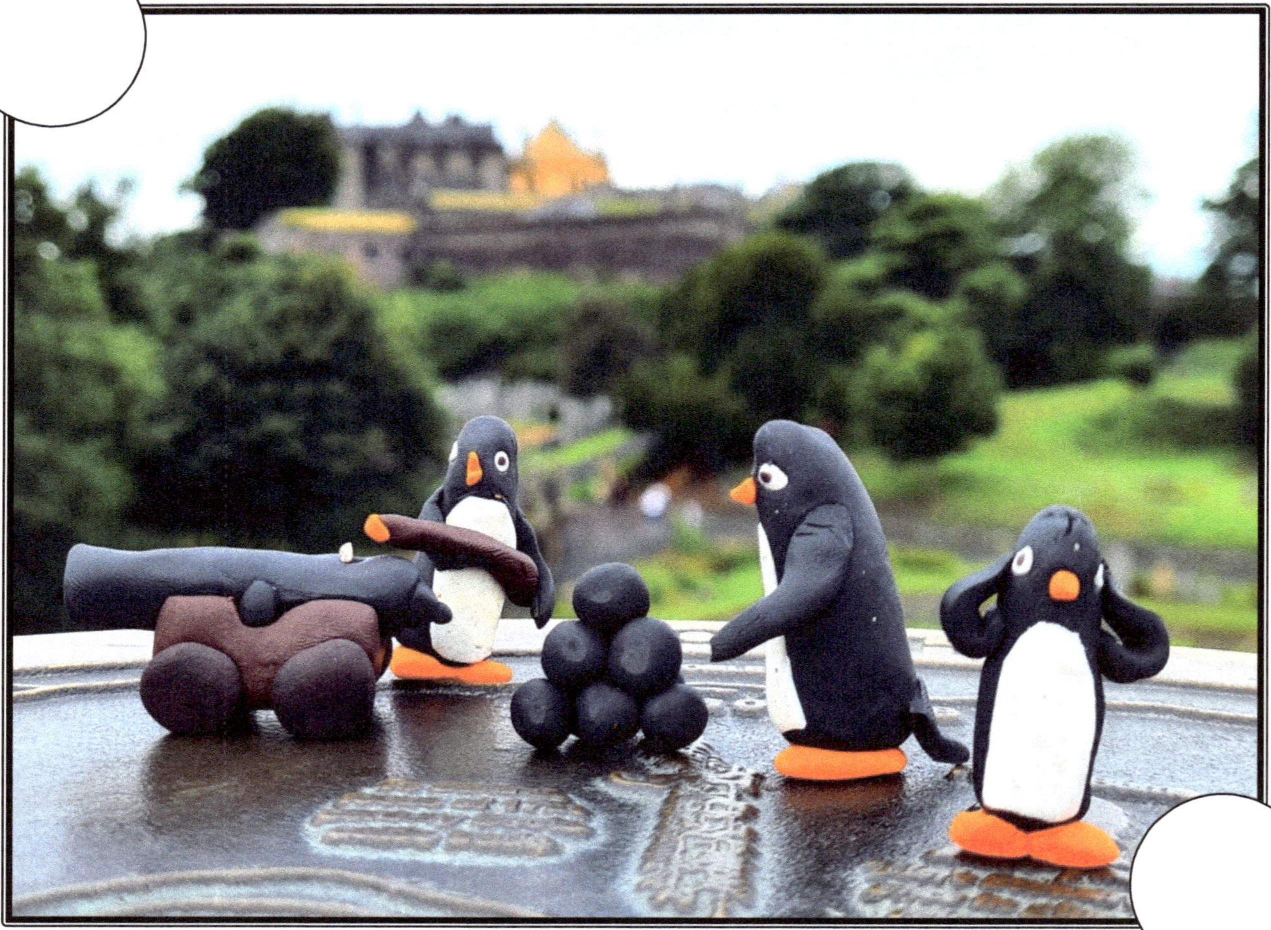

15th September 2023

This afternoon, we visited Stirling Castle, and we got to play around with a cannon (not a real one though!).

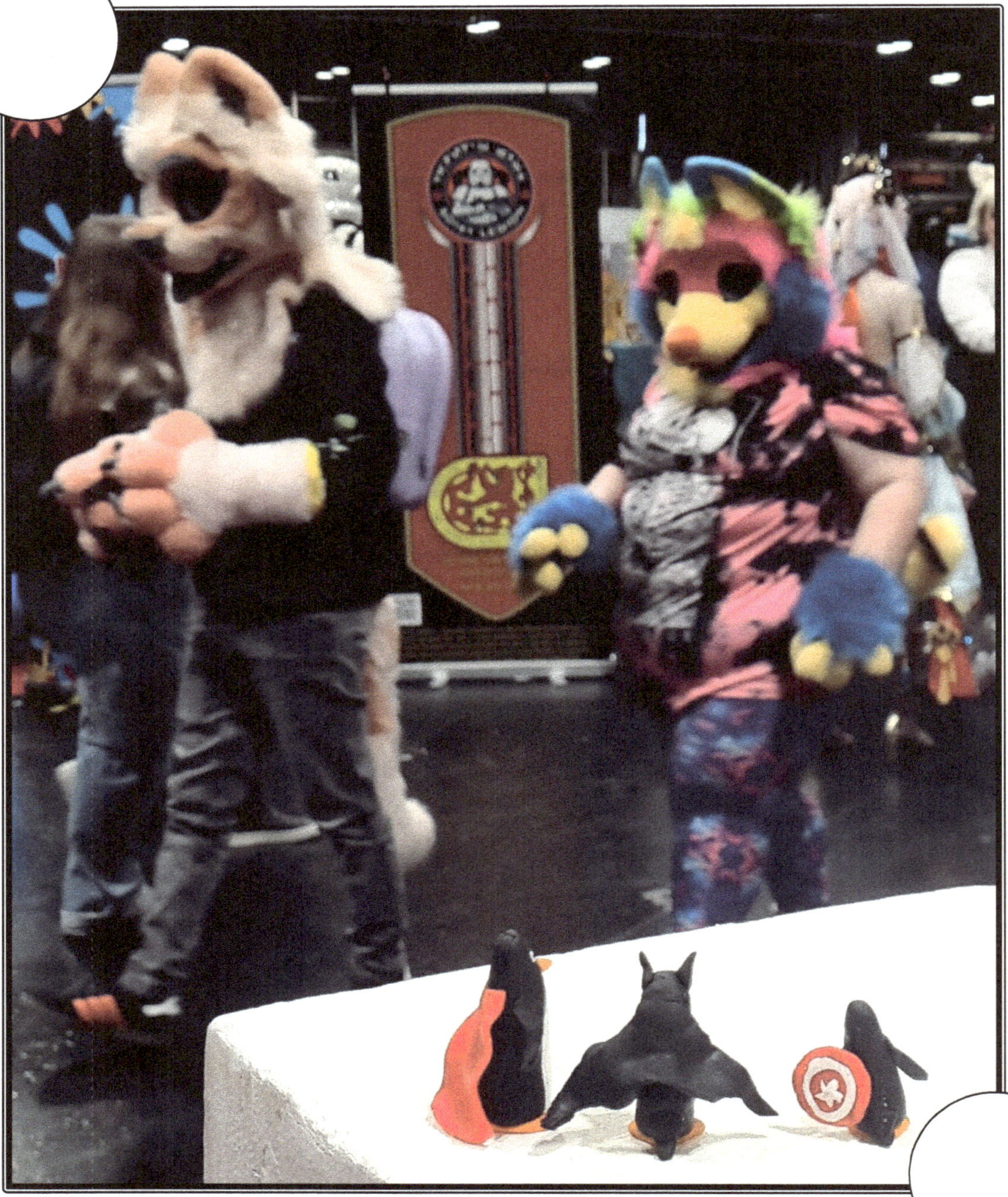

24th September 2023

Today we went to Comic Con at the
SEC in Glasgow! We dressed as superheroes.
Dad was Superman, my Little Brother was
Captain America and me, I'm Batman!

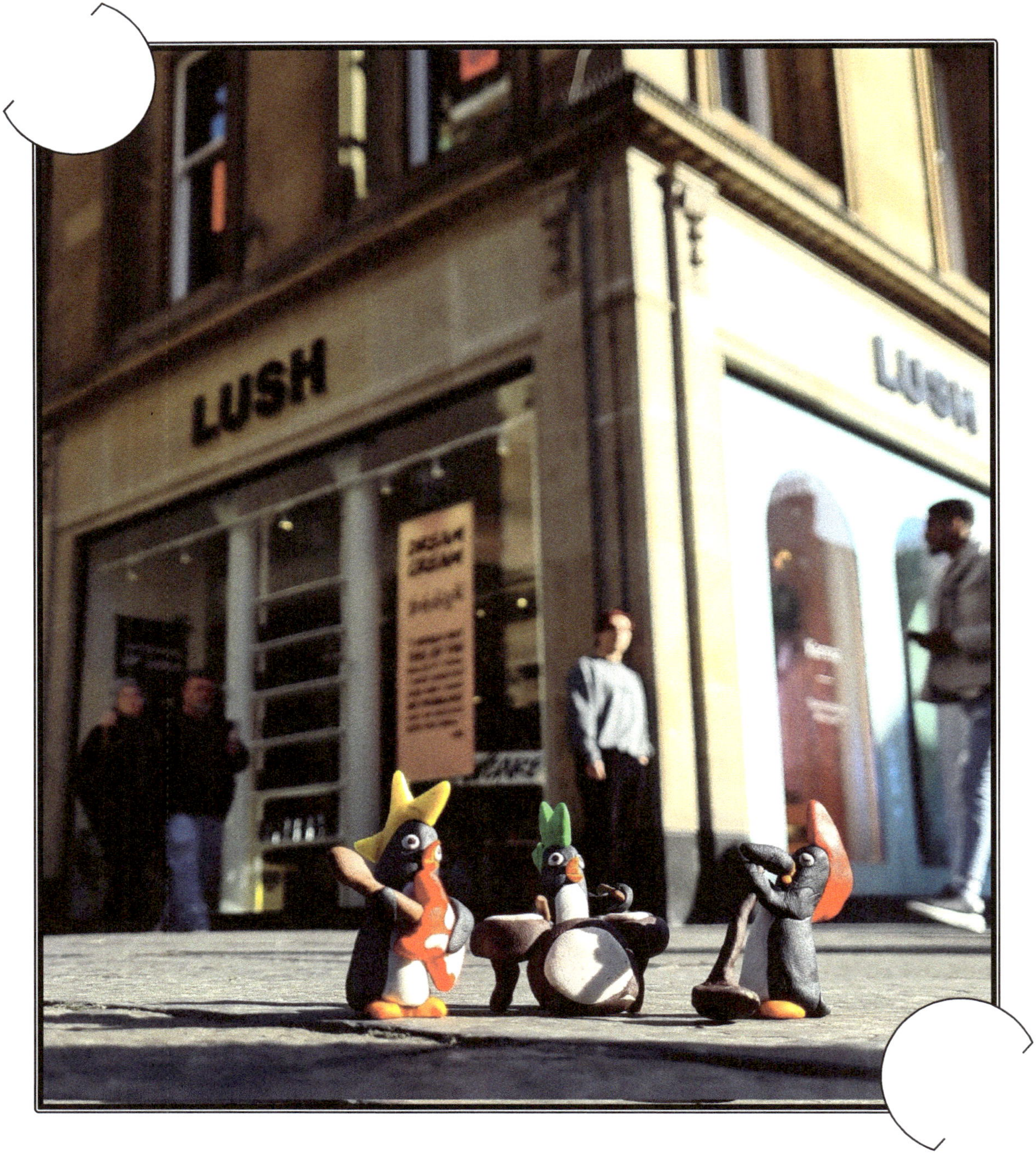
LUSH
LUSH

30th September 2023

The punks have formed a band,
and this weekend they went busking
on Buchanan Street in the centre of Glasgow.
We went along to listen to them, and unlike
Dad, they're actually very good musicians!

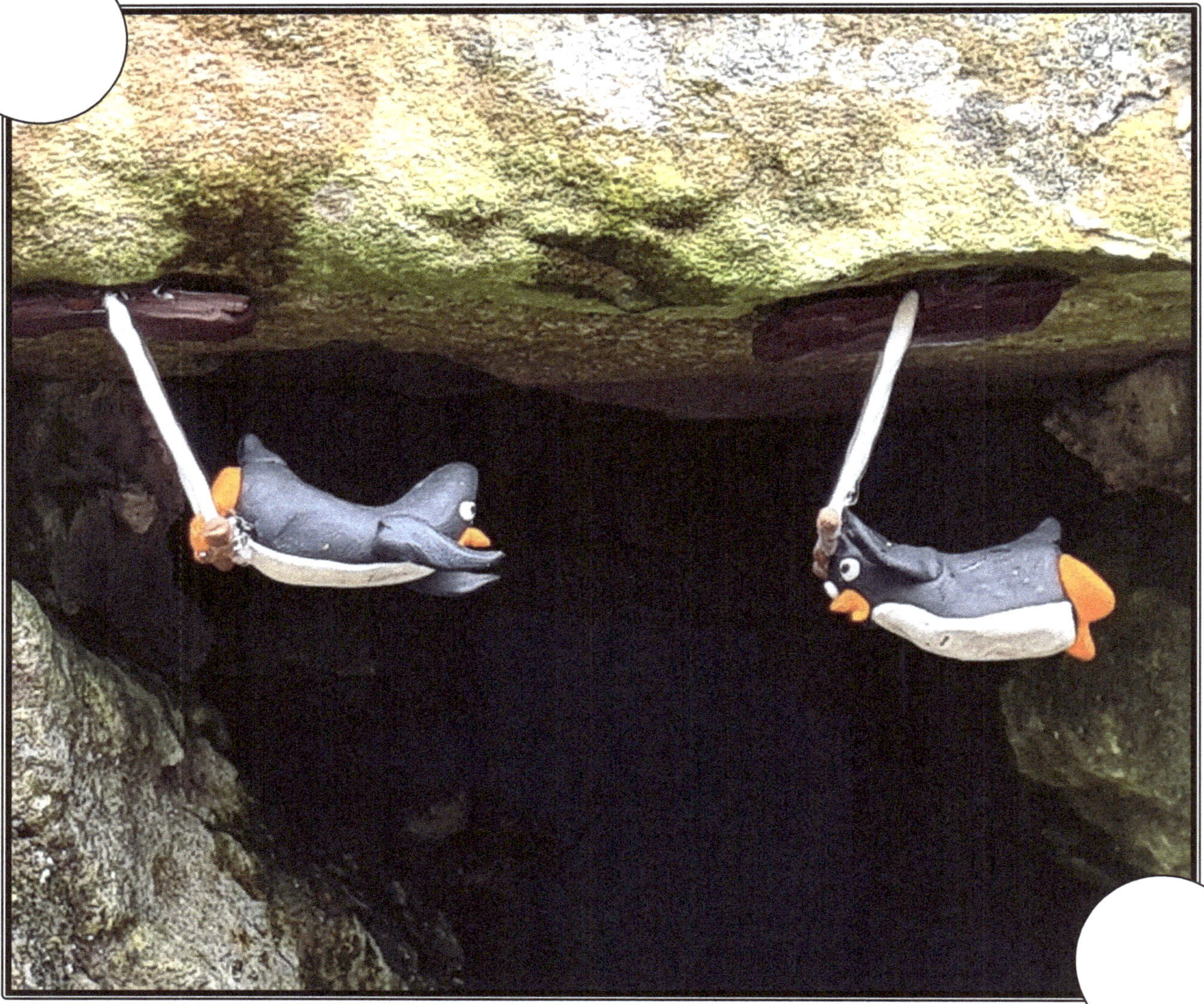

10th October 2023

Mum's not tried any new extreme sports in a while, so she spent this morning learning how to do the trapeze with one of her friends!

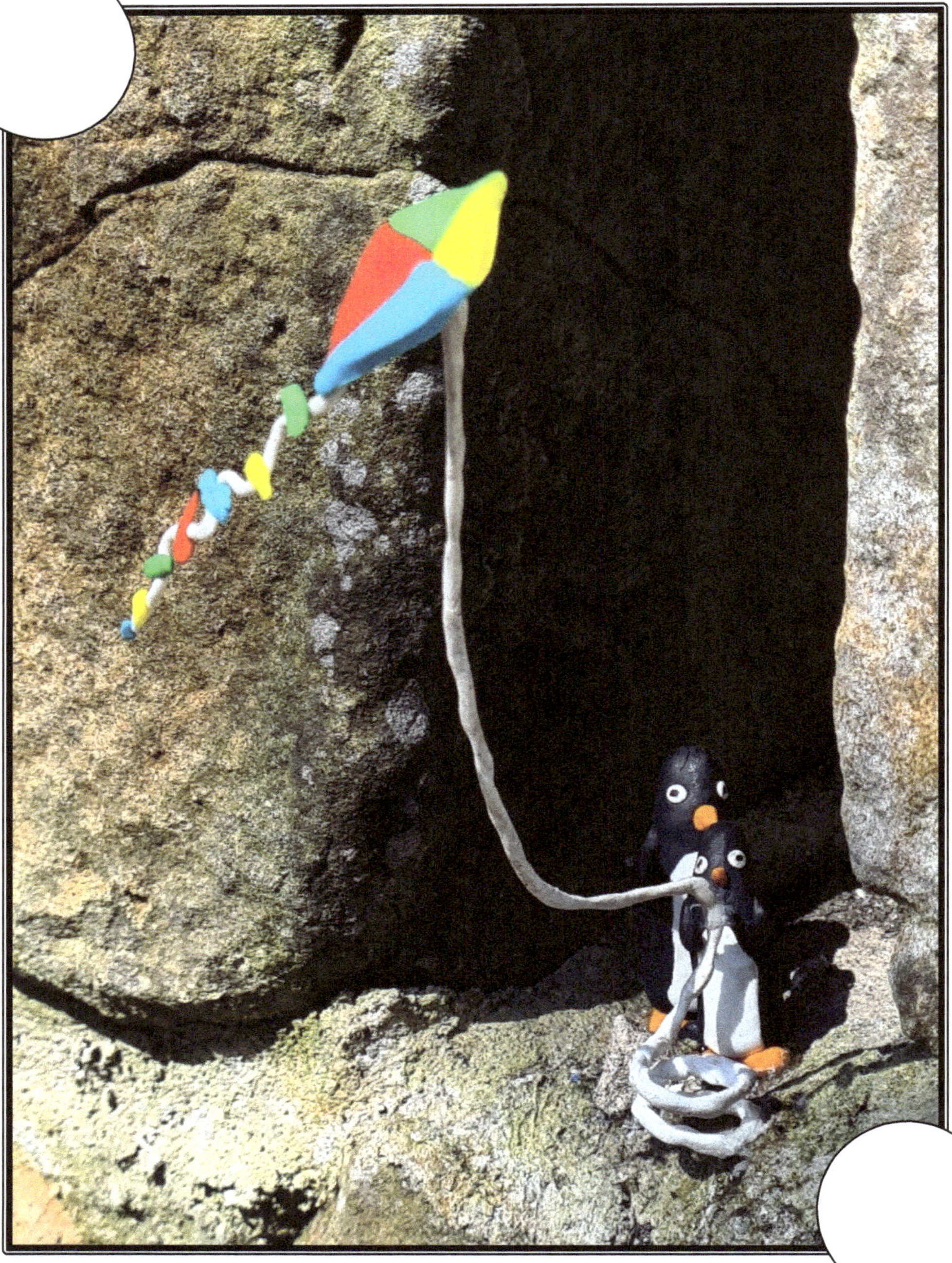

21st October 2023

Autumn is getting into full swing. This means the weather's not as good as it was in the Summer, but as it's now windier, Dad took me out and taught me to fly a kite!

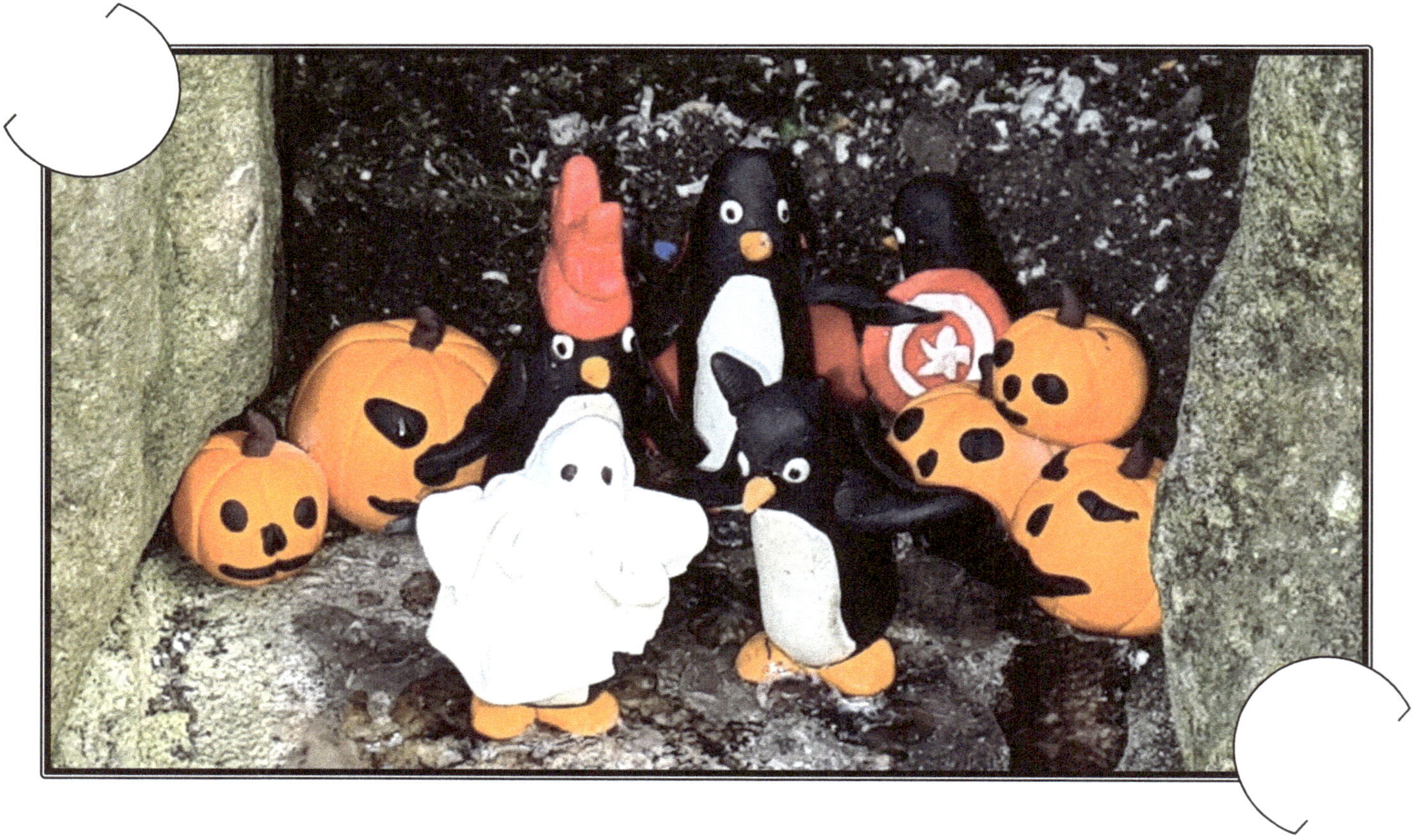

31st October 2023

It's Hallowe'en! And we're heading out to go trick-or-treating (or guising as it's called in Glasgow). My dad's wearing his Superman cape from Comic Con, my Mum's dressed as Feathers McGraw, My Little Brother's a ghost and of course, I'm batman!

Wait a minute, that's my Little Brother in the background with his Captain America shield! So who's the ghost then? How spooky!

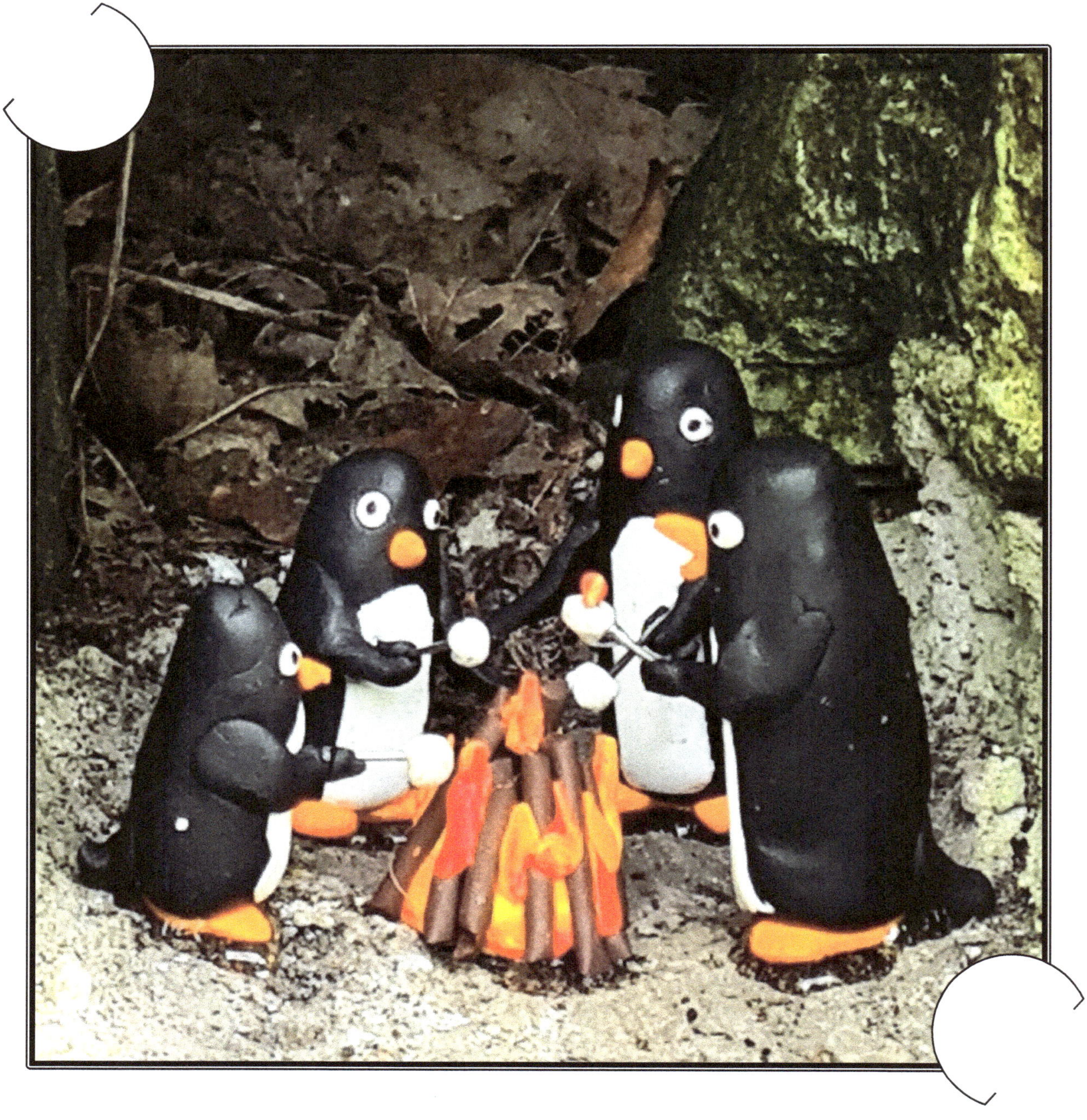

5th November 2023

As it's bonfire night, we made a campfire in the garden and roasted marshmallows over it as we watched the fireworks everyone else was setting off. As always, Dad set fire to his!

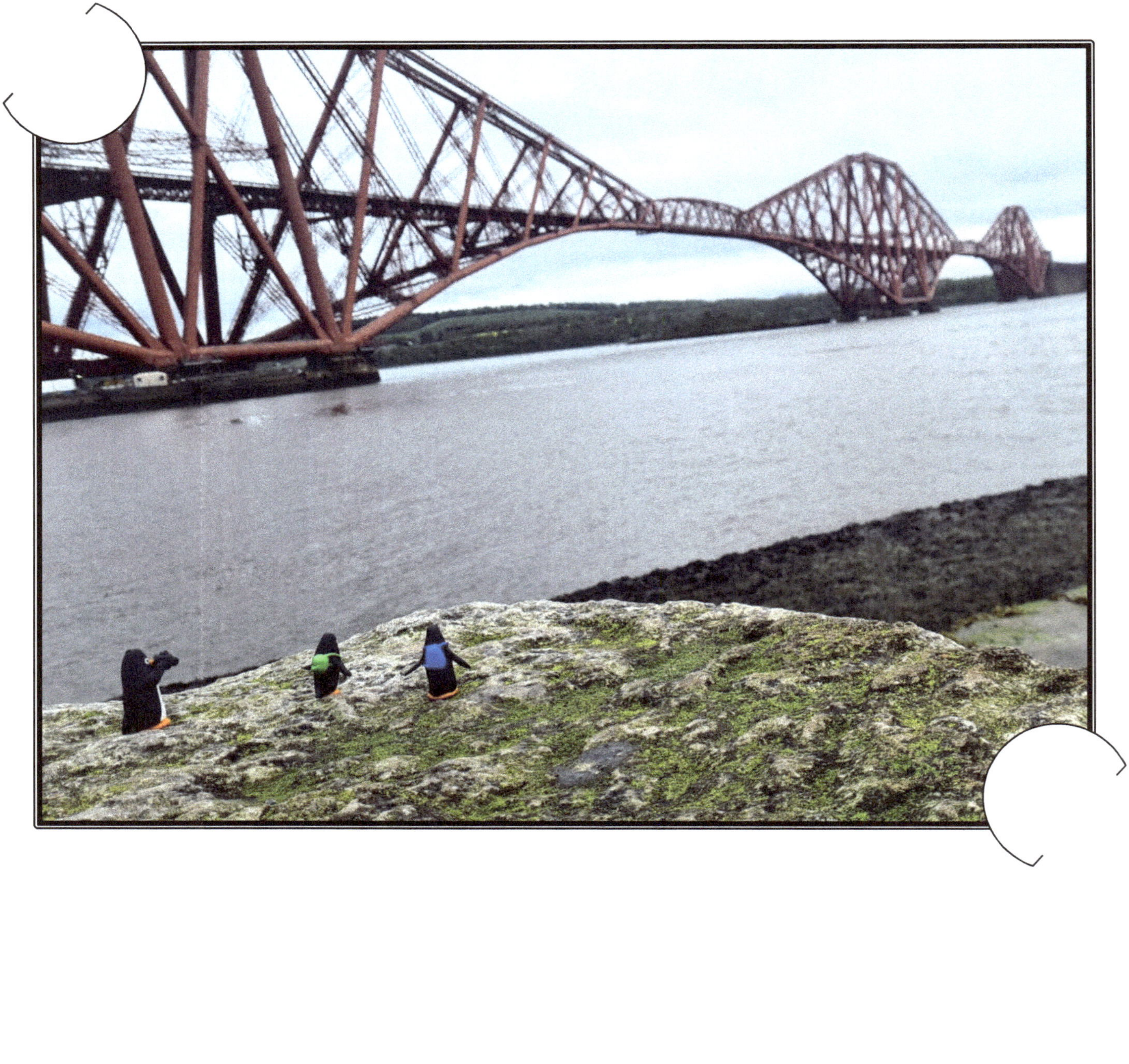

16th November 2023

The weather was surprisingly nice today,
so we went on a road trip. I don't know why,
but Dad's rather obsessed with bridges, so we
ended up at the Forth Bridge. I have to admit,
it's a very impressive bridge. My Dad said,
I wonder what the first three looked
like - he tells very bad
Dad jokes!

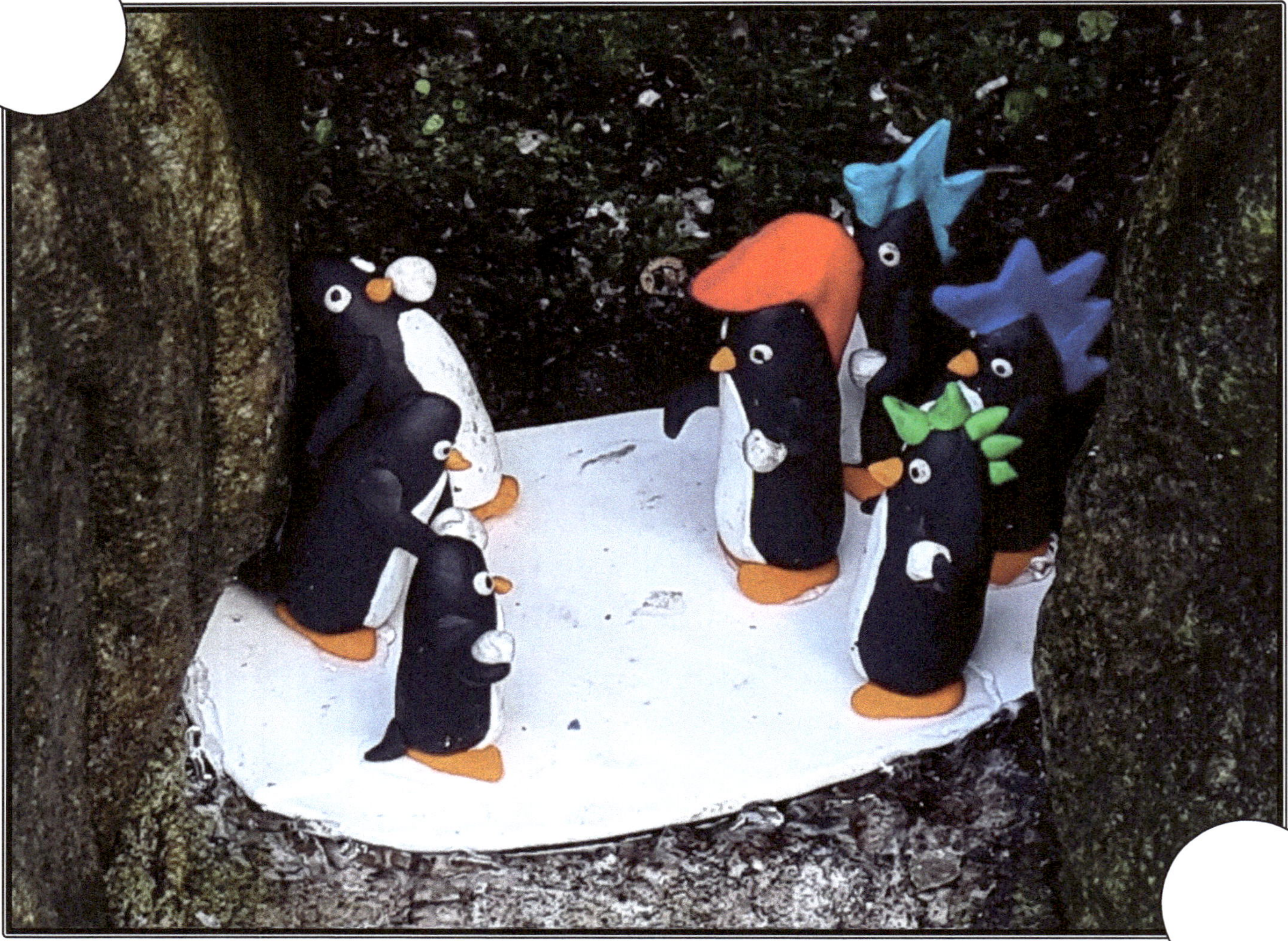

18th November 2023

It snowed last night, so I guess that means it's finally Winter again. Dad, me and my Little Brother took on the punks in a snowball fight. It was so much fun, especially when Dad got hit in the face by a snowball!

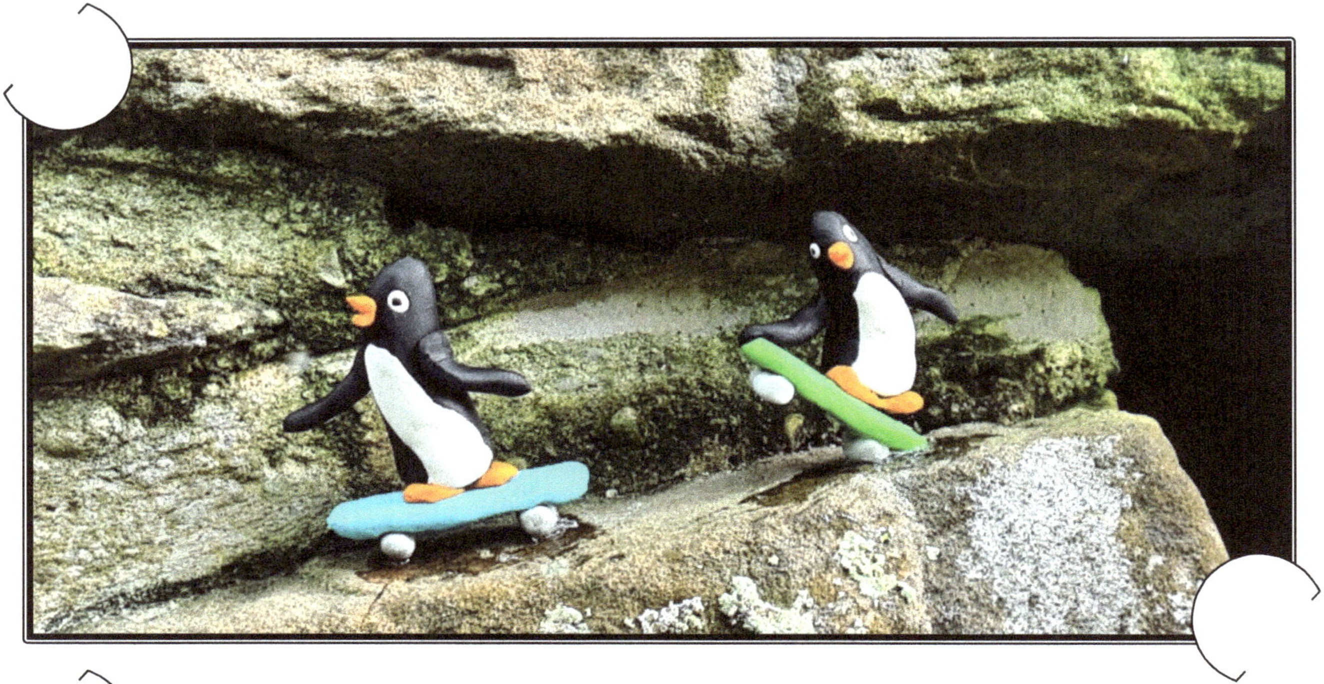

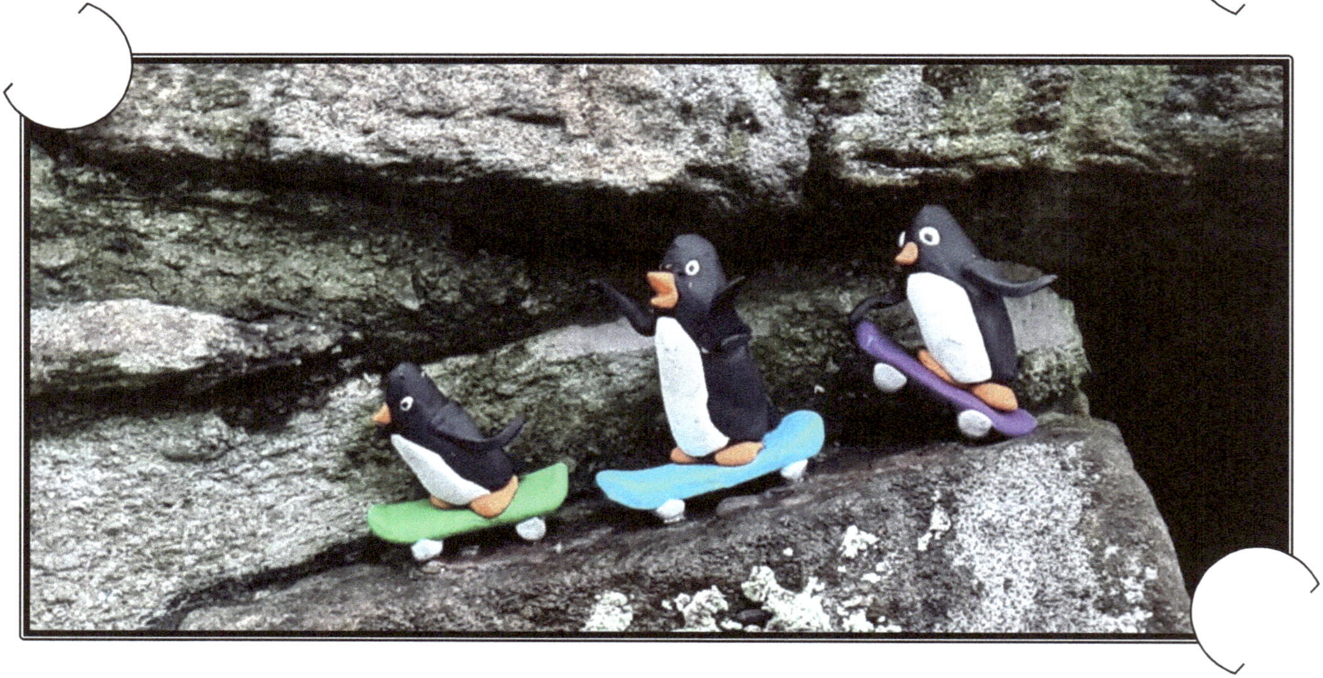

27th November 2023

Me and my Little Brother really like skateboarding. Once, we managed to persuade Dad to come with us. He screamed all the way down the hill!

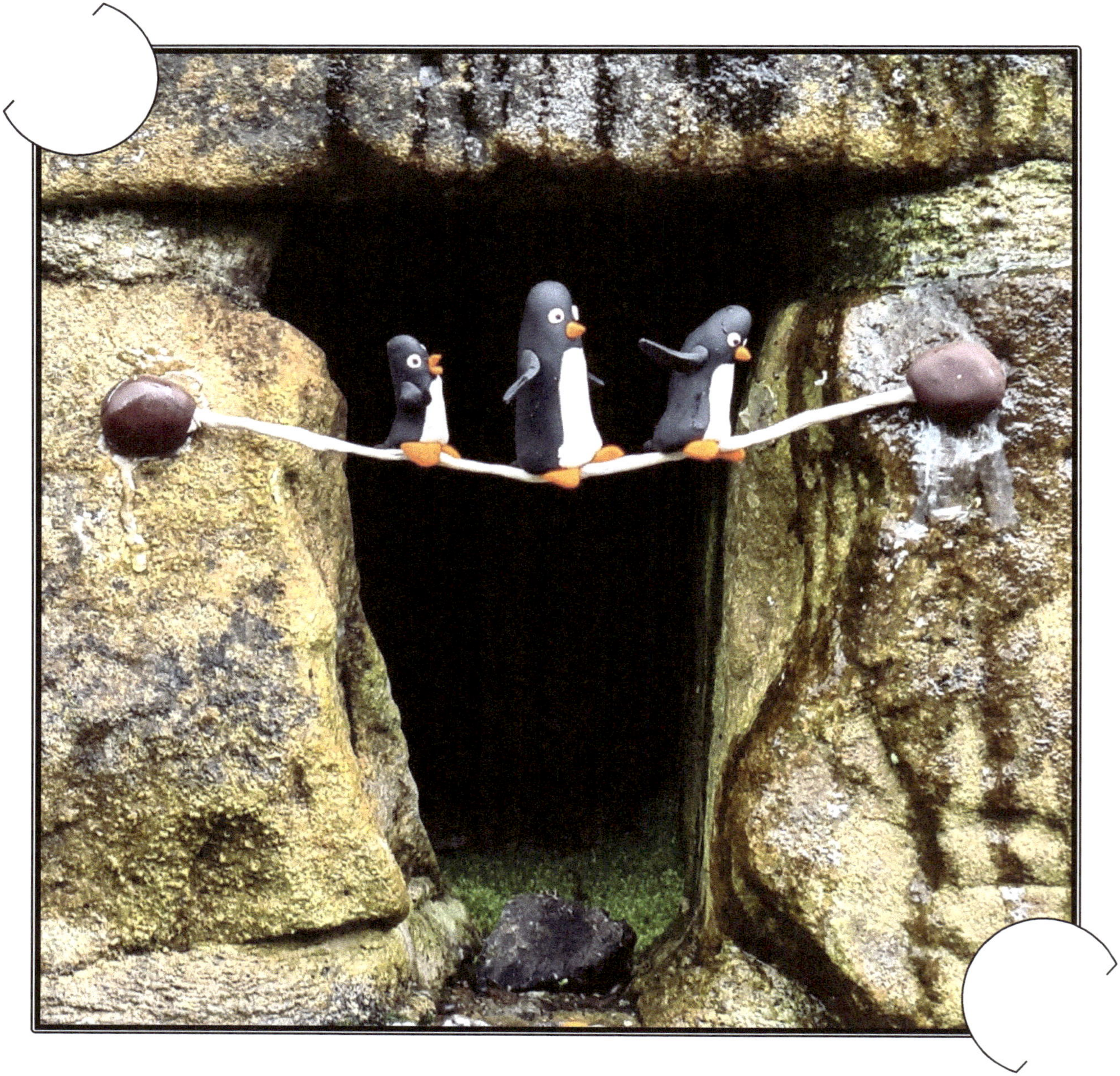

3rd December 2023

Mum decided it was about time me and my Little Brother learned how to do the tightrope. We both did it, but it's a lot scarier than it looks!!!

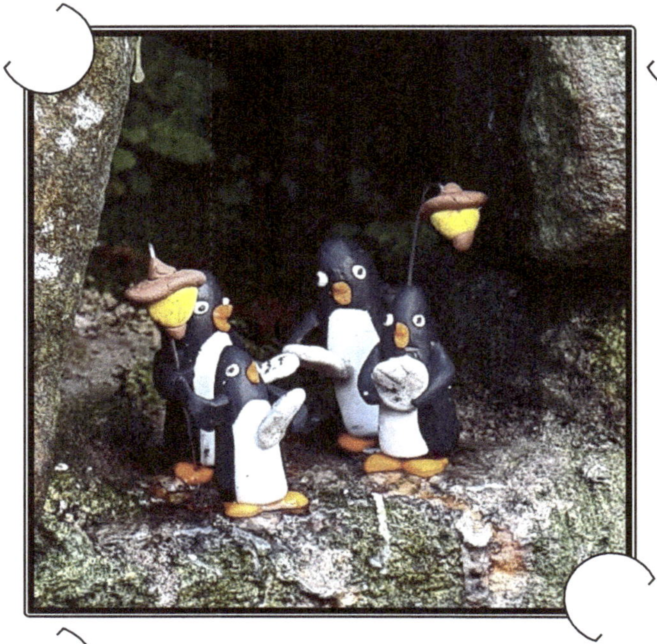

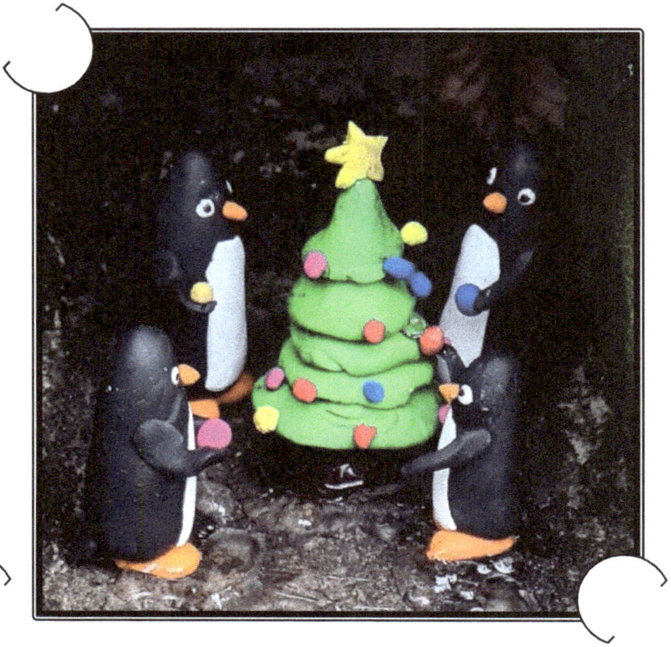

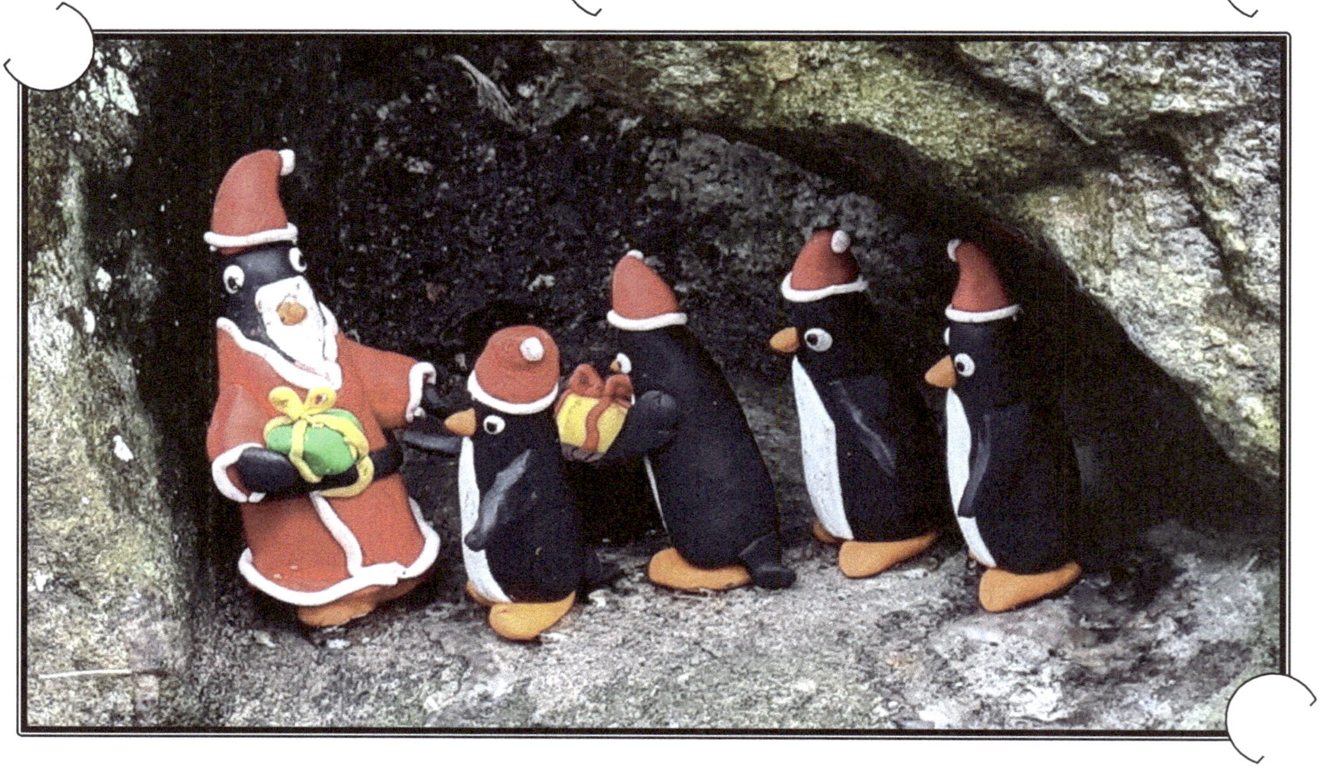

19th December 2023

Just like humans, we penguins celebrate Christmas. We sing carols, and decorate trees, and most importantly we get presents from Santa Claus - I REALLY hope mine's a mackerel this year!

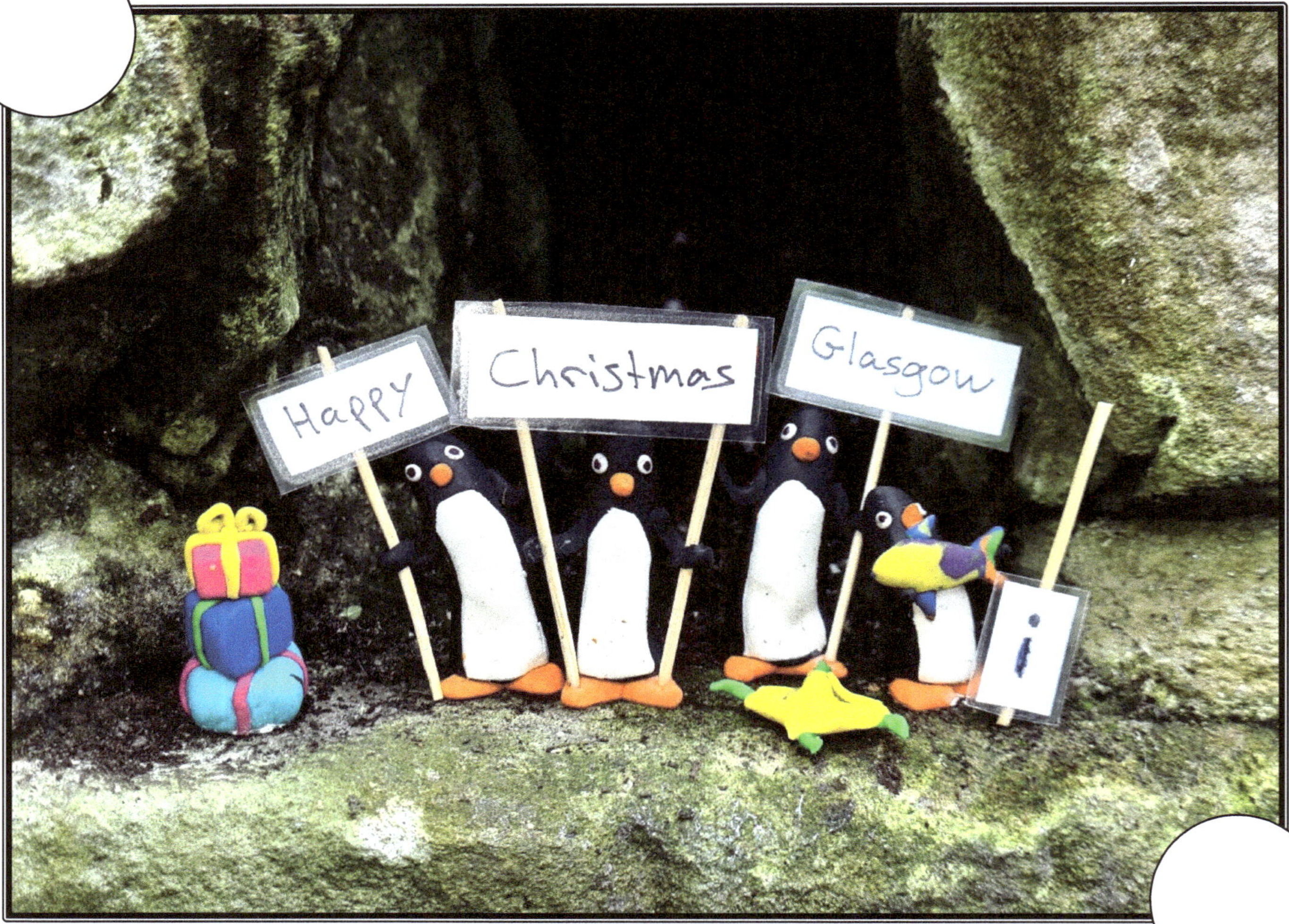
Happy
Christmas
Glasgow
!

25th December 2023

Happy Christmas, Glasgow!
Sorry my Little Brother couldn't wait until after the photo to open his present!

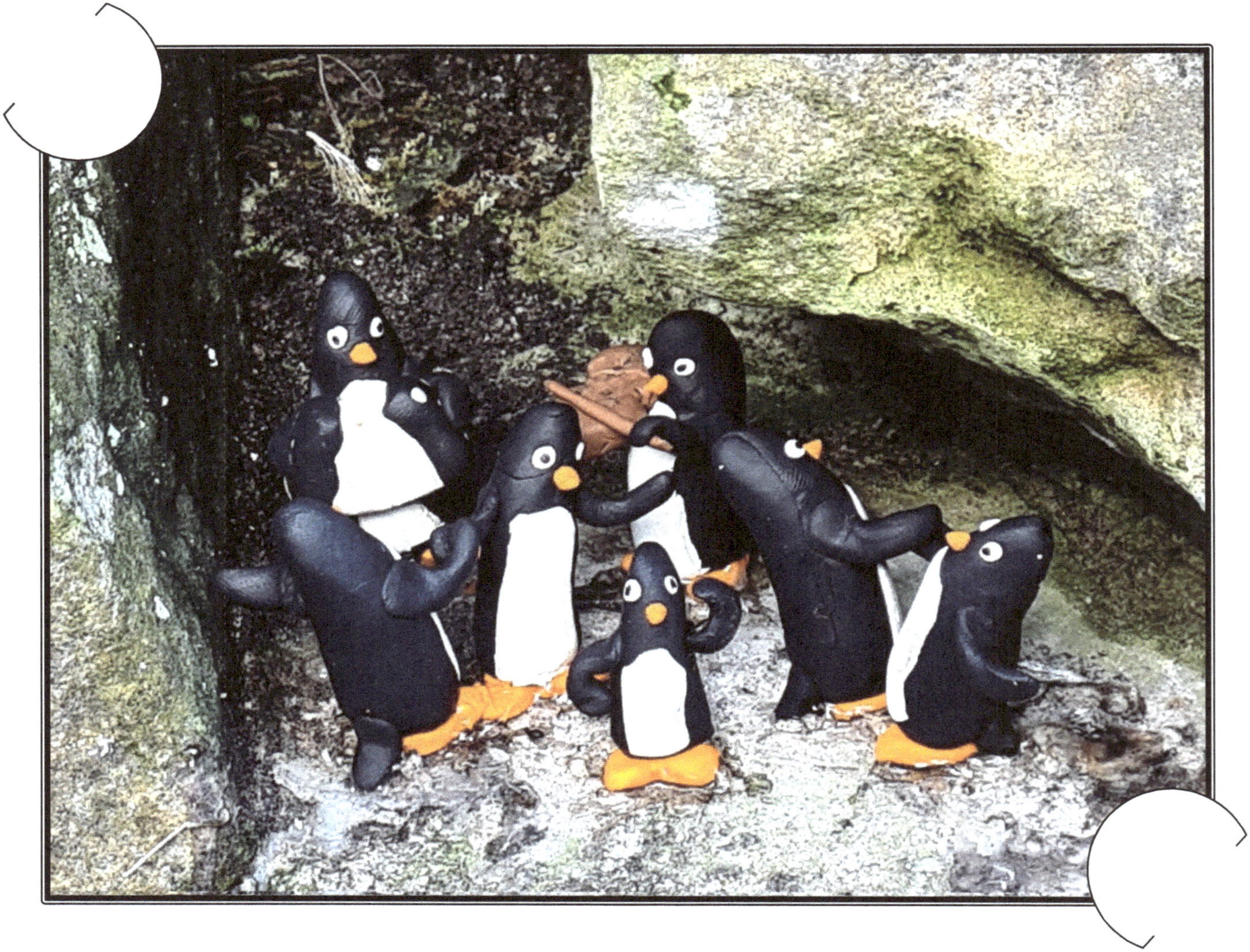

31th December 2023

We decided we should celebrate Hogmanay by having a ceilidh. This involved lots of Scottish music and dancing. That's Mum on the fiddle and my Uncle Finn on the accordion. They don't play together very often, but when they do, things can get really wild!

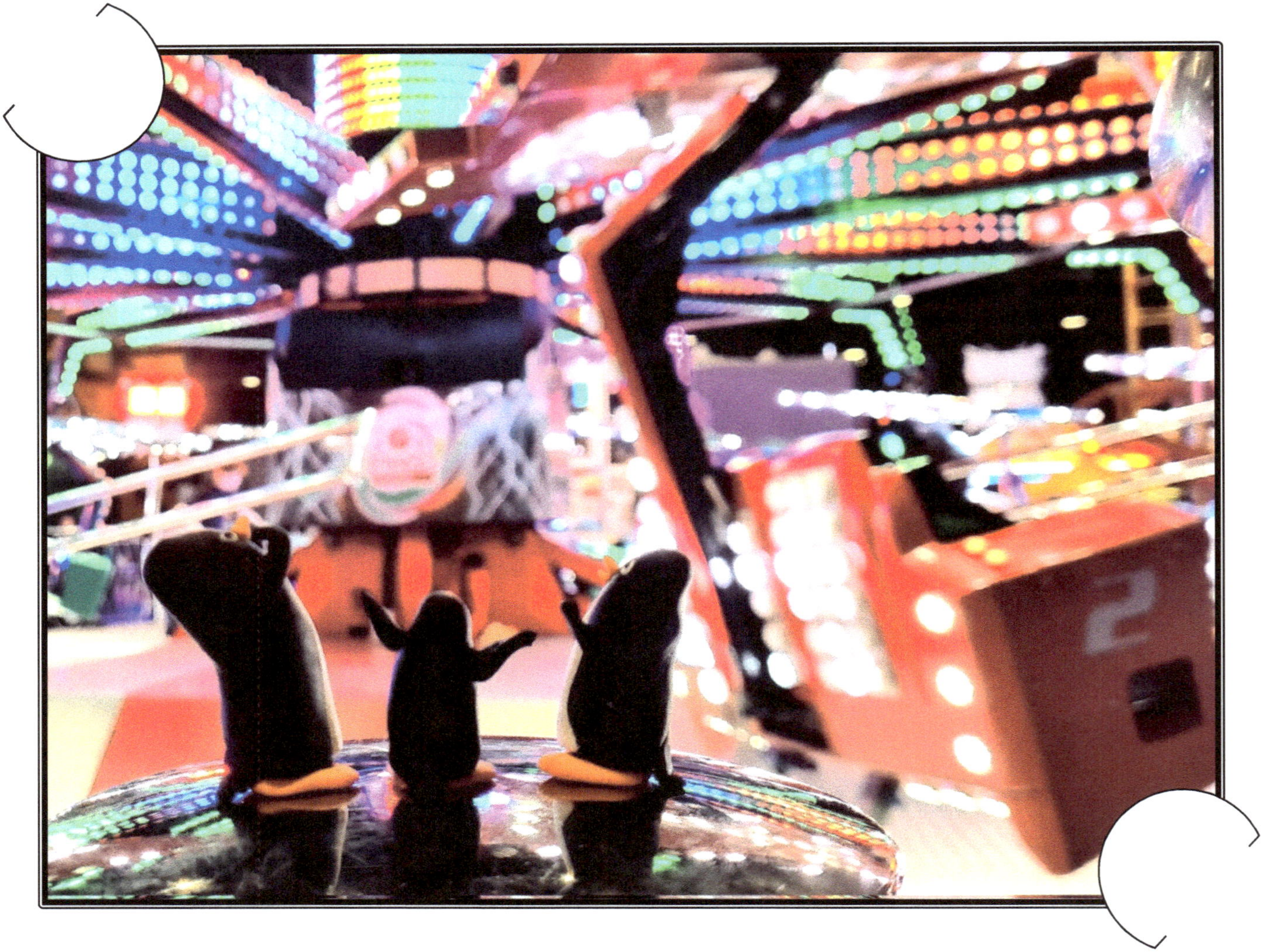

1st January 2024

Today we went to the Glasgow Carnival! We thought the rides were amazing, but Dad wasn't so keen on them!

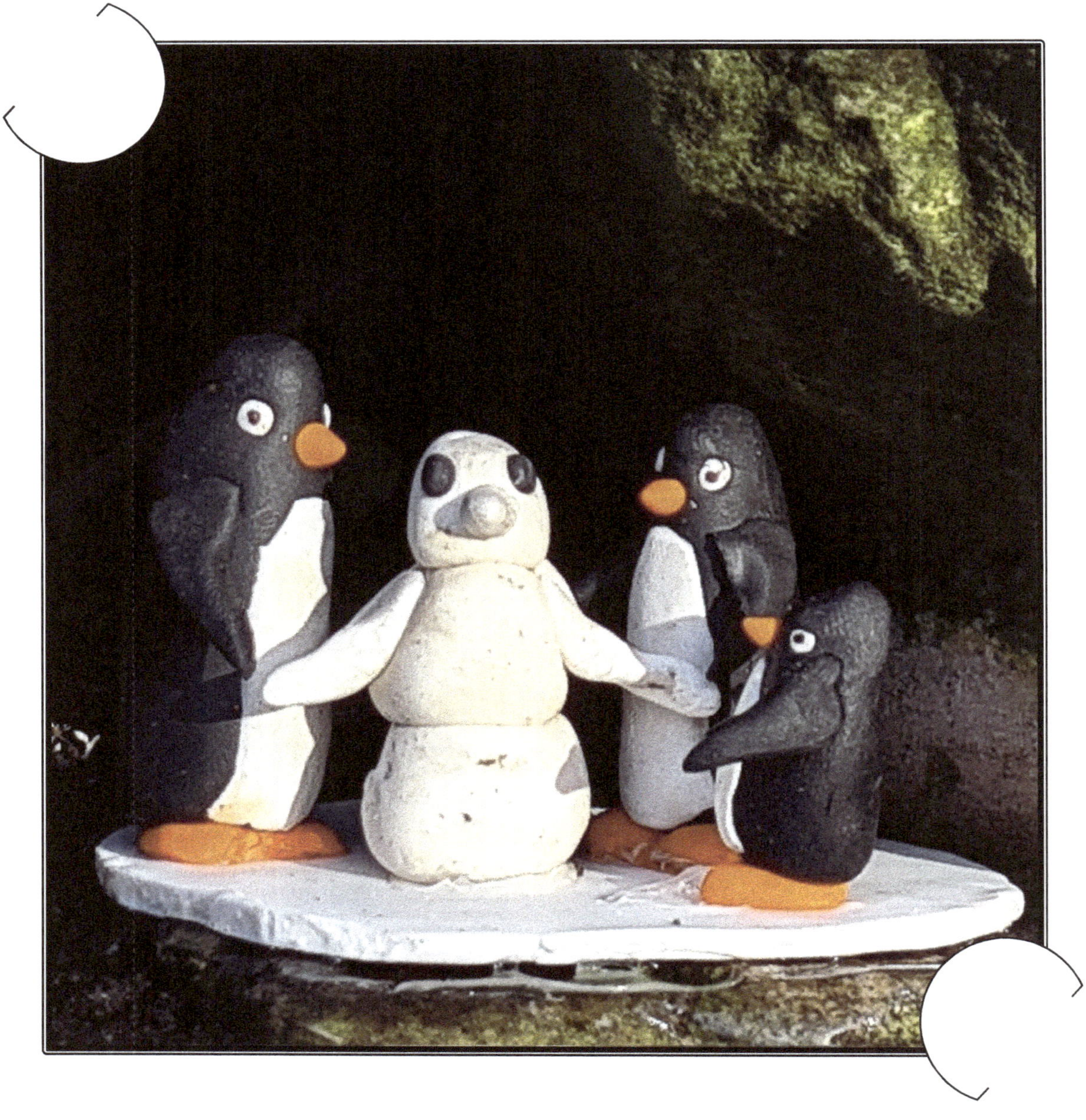

12th January 2024

It snowed again
today, so we made a
snow penguin!

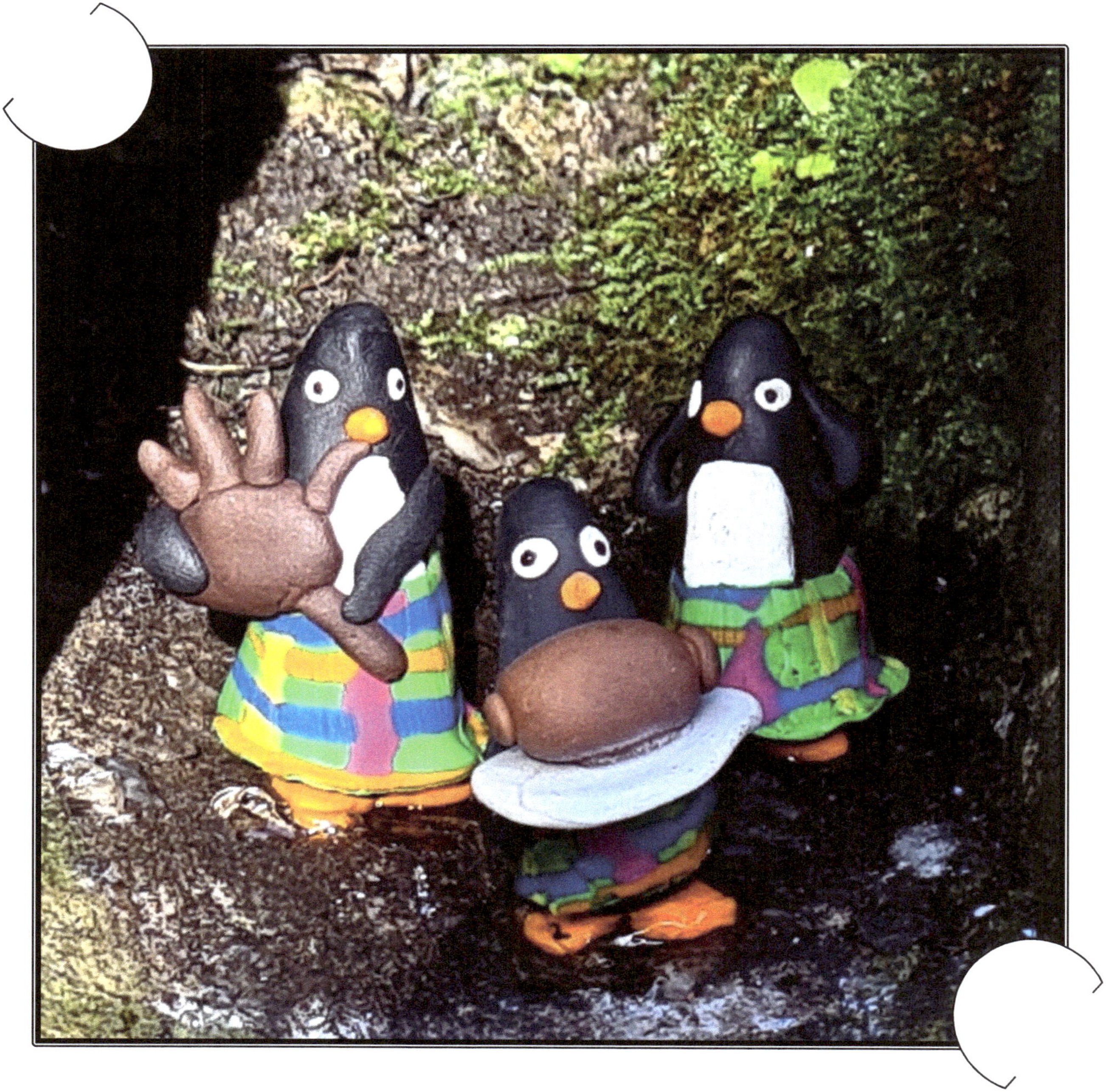

25th January 2024

It's our first Burn's Night in Glasgow, so we thought we'd try some haggis, but Dad insisted on piping it in. Despite all his practicing, his bagpiping REALLY hasn't gotten any better!!!

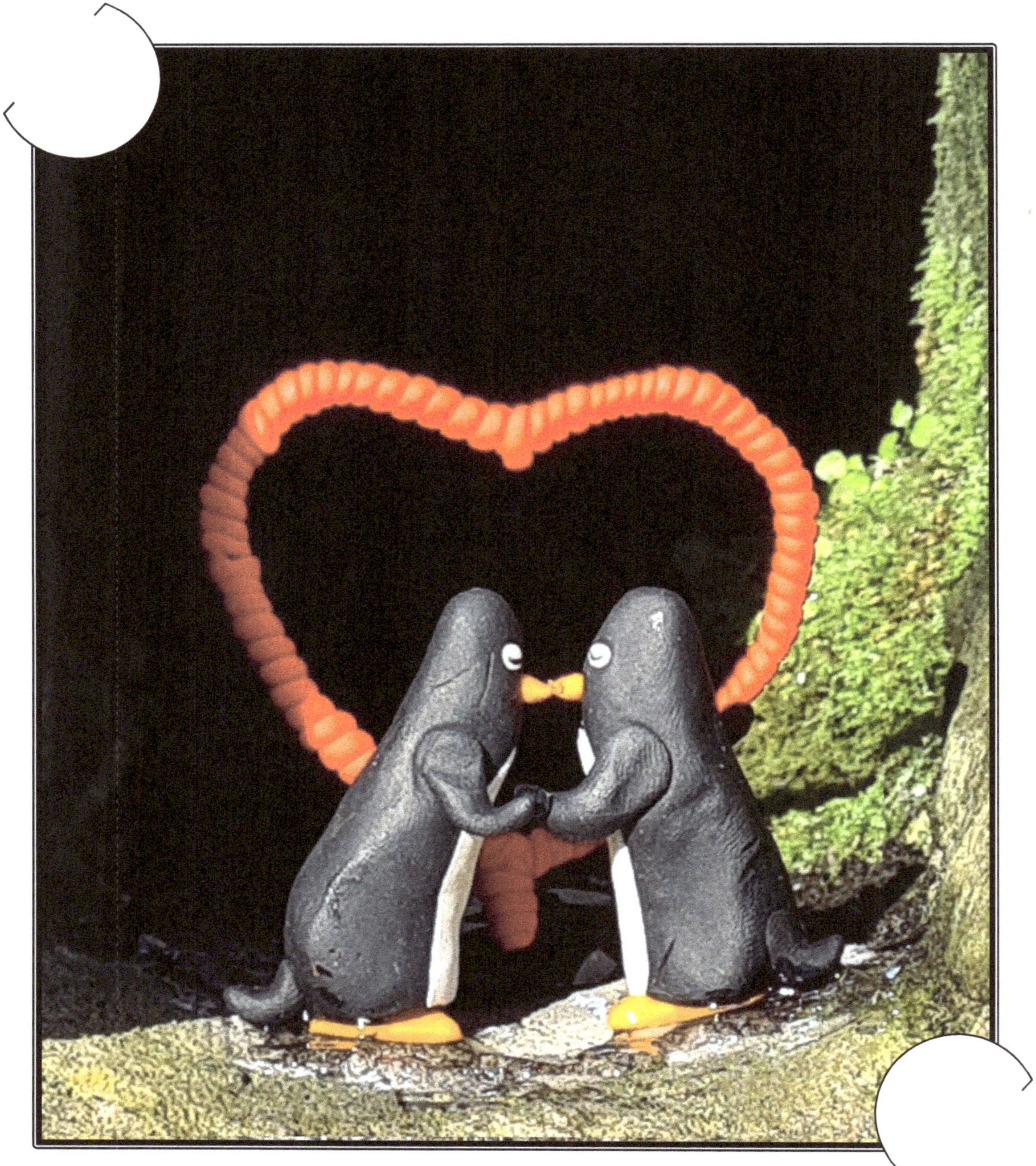

14th February 2024

Dad says Glasgow is the city of love
because Saint Valentine is buried here.
Mum says maybe this will mean he
won't have forgotten to get her
a card this year, like he's done
every other year!

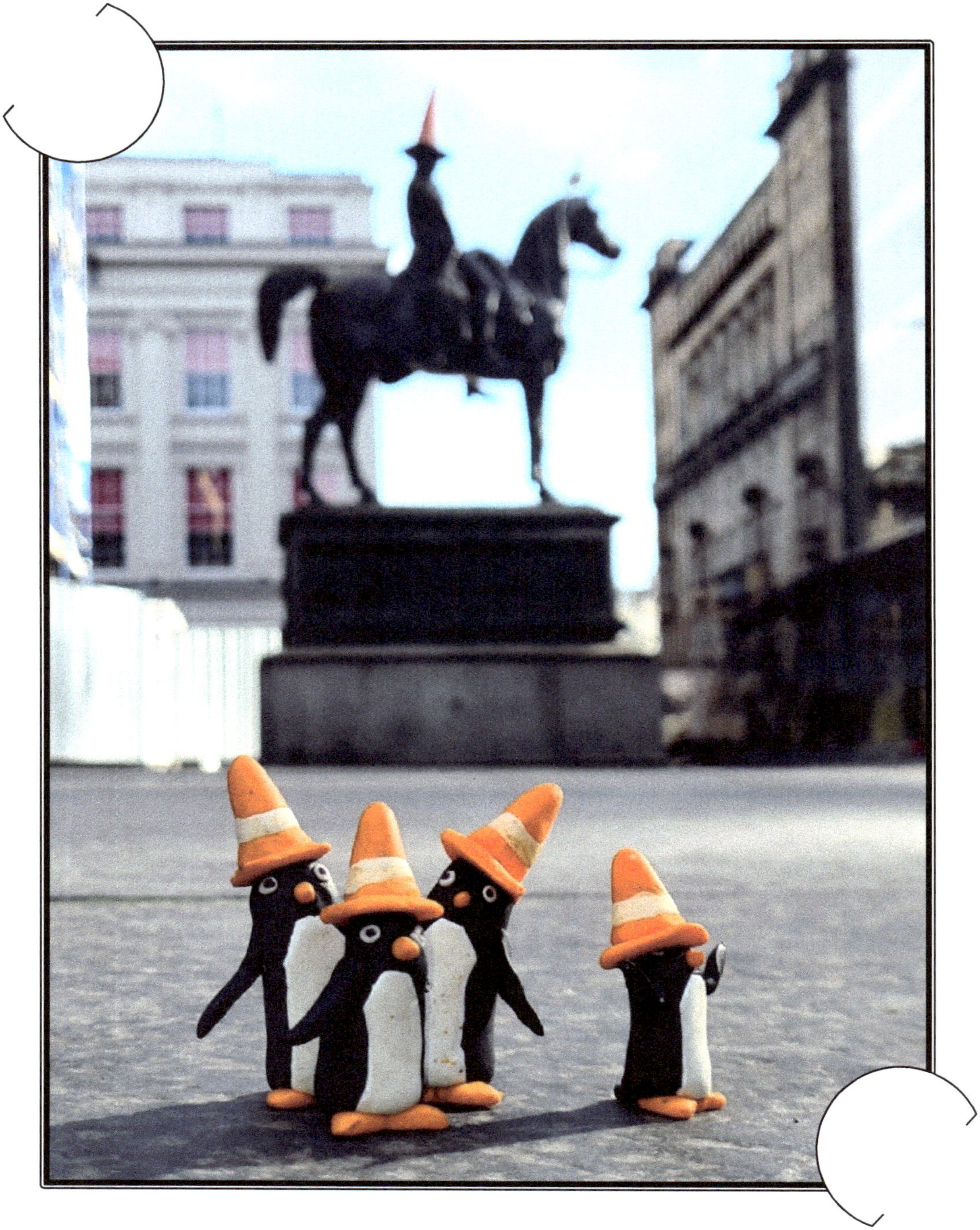

24th February 2024

We've now been in Glasgow for a whole year, and it only seemed right to celebrate by going to see the city's most famous statue. I don't know why he's wearing a road cone, but we thought we should wear them, too!

www.ingramcontent.com/pod-product-compliance
Ingram Content Group UK Ltd.
Pitfield, Milton Keynes, MK11 3LW, UK
UKHW051507060425
5330UKWH00073B/62
9 781909 832879